JOSEPH WHITFIELD

THE TREASURE
OF
EL DORADO

THE TREASURE
OF
EL DORADO

Featuring
"THE DAWN BREAKERS"

By JOSEPH WHITFIELD

Third Edition

Second Printing, 1984

OCCIDENTAL PRESS

Washington, D.C.   1981

6-86

Library of Congress Catalog Card No. 77-89125

ISBN 0-911-050-52-3

Printed in U.S.A.
APOLLO PRINTING and BINDERY
166 Main Ave · Passaic, N.J. 07055

Preface

Where should you turn when you seek for truth? You should turn within, where truth seeks you!

This is a story of the greatest treasure hunt in the history of Earth. It is a successful hunt. Never before has a treasure of greater magnitude been found.

This book is a chronicle of the discovery of the vast and virtually unrecorded Treasure of El Dorado; the legendary hoard that, before now, had been unsuccessfully sought for hundreds of years. You will find in this chronicle the revelations that led step by step to El Dorado's gold. It is a strange story. Oftentimes, it seems unrelated to treasure. In the end, you discover that the treasure is far greater than you could possibly have anticipated in the beginning.

The Author

Dedication

This book is dedicated to "The Dawn Breakers".

Who are "The Dawn Breakers"?

They are the ascended master teachers throughout the cosmos who serve God by helping to spiritually elevate their fellow man.

Since the beginning of time when the worlds of matter emerged from the higher vibrations of Divine Mind, the Dawn Breakers have brought the dawn of higher consciousness to those momentarily lost brothers who have chosen to experiment in the grosser physical vibrations such as Earth.

Who are "The Dawn Breakers"?

They are the members of the Divine Brotherhood who serve God by upraising a light and illuminating a world in darkness.

Glance through the following pages and you will see 16 paintings and sketches. They are likenesses of some of the Dawn Breakers, as seen by four psychic artists to whom they have appeared. The Dawn Breakers depicted here, along with many others, have appeared to the author to train him for his coming role of service to mankind.

The Dawn Breakers have instructed that none of the paintings or sketches be identified publicly. The reason they gave for this request was that, over the ages, too many people have become entrapped in personality worship, with the subsequent development of cultism and man-made religions. To the extent that people have become entrapped, they have been distracted from attaining their own cosmic self-realization. Since the whole purpose of this book is to aid individuals to attain self-realization, it will suffice for the paintings to appear in print without any identifying names.

Each painting or sketch carries its own powerful vibration which is designed to stimulate certain areas of one's subconscious. Although there will be many psychics around the Earth who will immediately recognize some of the masters depicted here, the author will neither confirm nor deny the actual identities. As the book itself reveals, each of us has many identities, so it is pointless, in a cosmic sense, to overemphasize a single personality.

This book is therefore dedicated with love to all of the Dawn Breakers who have come to help usher in a bright new dawn of consciousness to mankind in Earth.

The Author

Acknowledgment

Loving acknowledgment is hereby given to the four gifted artists who painted or sketched "The Dawn Breakers" pictured on the following pages. Three of the artists are known personally to the author. They are Gloria Allison of Miami, Florida, Rev. Norman E. Williams of Largo, Florida, and Irene Vores of Ft. Lauderdale, Florida. The fourth artist, Emilio Keutch Torres of Mexico, is not known personally by the author, but is an acquaintance of Gloria Allison.

In most instances, the artists themselves are not aware of the actual identity of the master or masters that they painted or sketched. It was usually a case in which the master or masters would appear to the artist who then was spontaneously inspired to record the impression.

In some instances, the author told the artist in advance that this would happen. In other instances the artist was inspired or directed to present the depicted master to the author. For example, the three paintings by Mr. Torres were presented to Mrs. Allison, who in turn was inspired to give them to the author, who recognized them as three of the masters who had instructed him!

As soon as the final draft of the manuscript was completed in February, 1976, the seven masters who are known as the seven Chohans of this solar system, appeared to the author. They instructed him to give a copy of the complete manuscript to Rev. Williams to read. They promised to appear to Rev. Williams as he read the manuscript and inspire him to sketch their likenesses for publication in this book. They kept their promise!

The Author

CONTENTS

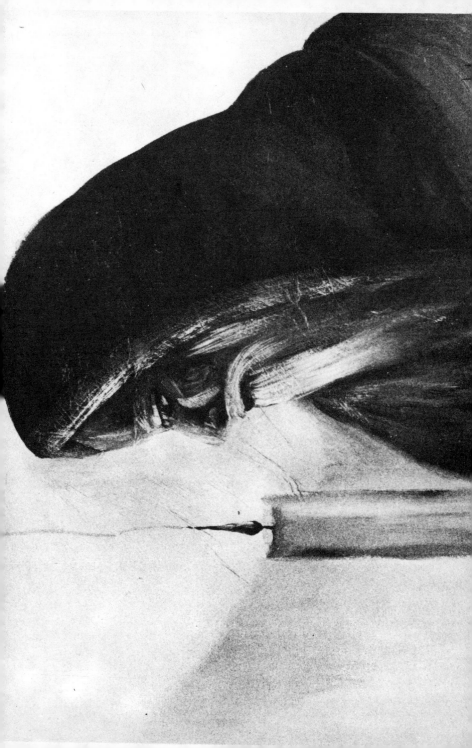

CHAPTER I

El Dorado Appears to Joseph

*Mental Communications
From Other Realms*

Unlearning Hurts

"Come, Joseph, I will lead you to my treasure!"

"Who are you?"

"I am El Dorado."

"El Dorado?"

"Yes."

"I hear your voice inside of my head, but I do not see you."

"This is mental communication or mental telepathy, Joseph. If you heed this voice I will guide you to the greatest treasure on Earth!"

"What treasure? What are you talking about?"

"These questions and much, much more will be answered, if you will but listen to the still small voice that I speak within you."

"I do not understand."

"You will, I assure you. Be patient. The time has arrived for this great treasure to be shared with mankind. In the past, men have searched in vain for the Treasure of El Dorado. Many have come very close to finding it. Some, indeed, have recovered parts of it and enriched themselves greatly, but until now no one has discovered the entire treasure."

Thus began a relationship that was to lead me through a painful process of unlearning and learning, before the fabled, legendary and virtually immeasurable Treasure of El Dorado could finally be entrusted to me.

Human nature being what it is, I was extremely excited by the lure and vision of a huge treasure. The possibility of having virtually limitless wealth with which to satisfy my benevolent nature as well as my selfish whims filled me with nervous expectancy. I found myself impatiently awaiting El Dorado's next contact. I had to wait seven days. Finally the voice spoke again inside my head.

"Hello, Joseph. This is El Dorado."

"I am certainly glad you have returned, El Dorado! I was almost beginning to think that I had imagined our first encounter. Would you please answer some questions for me?"

"I will answer your questions, Joseph, for I know the wonderment that is encompassing your mind. It will be necessary to clarify much as we go along, so ask me your questions."

"First, El Dorado, I want to know what is happening to me and why it is that I can suddenly hear mental communications?"

"You have picked a very good place to start, Joseph. Mental communication is a natural ability that all men possess, although it is seldom developed to any high degree by people in Earth. People of Earth have been so physically grounded in the past that most of them have relied almost exclusively on their five physical senses to the neglect of their higher spiritual, or psychic, faculties.

"The reason that you can 'hear' me is that I possess the spiritual power to overcome the limitations of the physical dimensions. What is happening to you is that you have been seeking to develop your spiritual capacities. You have been searching for answers. You have been motivated in this search by a sincere desire to help mankind. My coming to you is a natural result of the positive forces that you have put into motion by your positive thinking and your genuine desire to serve mankind. The heavens are filled with beautiful beings awaiting the opportunity to work through willing channels on Earth.

"What is happening to you is really no different than what happened to the prophets of the Old Testament or others of Earth's great inspired Scriptures.

"What do you mean by that?"

"Think for a moment, Joseph. Just where do you suppose that the prophets received the information that formed the basis for their prophecies? If you will just glance through the books of prophecy that comprise the Old Testament, you will find the following statements repeated once or more in different ways by the various prophets:

> "And the Lord said to me."
> "And the Lord spoke to me again."
> "The word of the Lord came to me."
> "Thus saith the Lord."
> "For the Lord God doth nothing without revealing his secret to his servants the prophets."
> "And the word of the Lord of Hosts came to me saying."

"And the angel that spoke in me, said to me."

"All of these statements are but references to telepathic communication. Within the framework and context of those bygone days, the prophets would quite naturally have looked upon this occurence as a 'miracle' coming directly from 'God'! Actually it was no more a miracle than what is now happening to you. In the present, as in the past, these communications are taking place all over Earth. Many individuals and groups are currently receiving and recording these communications which cover a wide range of information. The term most frequently applied to this form of communication is channeling. In the months that lie ahead, you would do well to prepare yourself to receive my great treasure by seeking out and reading some of the channelings that are being received in Earth. You must do this to understand fully what is taking place upon Earth, and why.

"There are many highly spiritual individuals and groups who are bringing forth and publishing important information received mentally from beyond Earth. To gain the broadest possible understanding, it would be wise to expose yourself to the full spectrum of this information. If you do this, you will soon note that there is an astonishing similarity of channeled data coming from widely separated individuals and groups. And many of these channels are unaware of the existence of others receiving similar messages. This in itself is a form of verification to sincere people seeking the truth.

"Bear in mind that you are not to limit or restrict yourself to one source, for the answers come from many sources. No one person or group has a monopoly on truth, and within all persons and groups there is some degree of error. It is only by exposing yourself to a broad spectrum as I have suggested that you will be able to properly discern what is truth and what is error.

"Meanwhile, in the course of my instructions we will cover enough material to give you a broad overview of the changes taking place upon Earth and within our solar system along with the reasons for these changes. From time to time I will introduce you to other masters who will deliver specialized discourses on subjects of great importance. All of this you are to record in a suitable manner. At the appropriate time you will then compile certain of these discourses along with certain experiences that you will be having, and you will publish a book that will change the cosmic understanding of mankind upon Earth.

"A word of caution! In your quest for further illumination, do not ever permit yourself to be overly influenced or dominated by any individual personality or group. To the extent that you become too attached or too engrossed in any group or individual teaching, you may find yourself becoming entrapped which will severely limit your growth. Since you already have the personal experience of becoming almost totally involved with religion, you can readily understand the reasons for these suggestions.

"It is also important for you to understand that all psychic abilities and expressions are a form of channeling."

"I'm not sure that I understand what you mean. Would you give me some examples?"

"I know of your interest in so-called psychic or spiritual healing. This is a form of channeling. If you were to ask most healers how the healing takes place they would answer you something like this, "God works through me," or "God sends this current through me," or "the Holy Spirit flows through me," or something similar. Of course, they are all correct in the sense that all things stem from the One Source usually referred to as God or Spirit. But what is literally and actually taking place in every instance is a form of channeling whereby an entity or entities from a realm other than (physical) Earth is directing certain corrective vibrations through the body, mind, soul and emotions of the healer (or channel) into the person being healed."

"I'm going to have to think about that. I find it difficult to accept or understand at this time."

"You will be exposed to much in the days ahead that will be very difficult for you to accept. Nothing will be forced upon you. I do not expect you to accept everything that is given. However, I do expect you to keep an open mind. That which you cannot accept at the moment, do not reject. Set it aside for a time. Later you may find that it makes a great deal of sense in the light of subsequent revelations."

"Can you give me some other examples of channeling?"

"Inventing is a form of channeling. Many of Earth's greatest inventions are channeled through the 'inventor' by a technique which we describe as mental imagery projection. In this technique, an actual picture is projected through the subconscious mind of the 'inventor' into the conscious mind, producing a vibration within the consciousness. The conscious mind translates the projected vibration into a picture image in much the same way as a television set translates and reproduces a projected image vibration.

"Another form of channeling is the composition of music. Music, in fact, is one of the most important areas in which we work. Through music, we are able to introduce into Earth's ethers various sound patterns and vibrations. In turn, these sound patterns and vibrations produce corresponding changes in mankind and in everything else upon Earth. Sound affects everything in your life—your emotions, your mental well-being, the equilibrium of body as well as your subconscious functioning. Sound combinations can and do affect the rate of progress and change that is ushering mankind from the dark ages into the new age.

"Other forms of channeling are creative writing and art. I need hardly stress the importance of both in man's development. Still other forms of channeling are those techniques normally associated with the occult such as clairvoyance, clairaudience, clairsentience, trance mediumship, palmistry, astrology, tarot reading, spirit photography and others. These examples should place in your mind the concept and the reality that channeling is a cooperative effort, a joint venture, involving man of Earth with entities beyond the physical dimensions. This is the truth. The sooner that you and others of Earth begin to realize these facts, the sooner and smoother will be Earth's progress into the New Age.

"The degree of one's sensitivity to the non-physical realms determines the degree to which higher ideas and concepts can be successfully channeled into Earth."

"I'm beginning to understand, El Dorado. How does one go about becoming more sensitive?"

"The first step, Joseph, is desire. The second is simply to learn to sit still and listen. The third is patience. The fourth is cooperation. The fifth is discernment."

"As you know, El Dorado, I have been practicing meditation for several years. I presume that this is what you mean when you say 'to sit still and listen'."

"Yes, that is correct. It should be mentioned, however, that one should not limit oneself in this respect by relying upon certain formulas or mantras or secret words and sounds or reliance upon a guru or upon group meditation. These are restrictions which tend to inhibit the results which meditation promises to provide.

"It is necessary that I expound a bit upon the importance of and necessity for discernment. Many individuals, when they begin to explore the psychic for the purposes of communication, make serious errors of discernment. They assume, while in communication with a being from another realm, that this being has a greater knowledge, greater wisdom, a more expanded consciousness than they do. Remember that an entity or an individualization who is on a plane or dimension, other than an Earth manifestation, is not necessarily in a purer or a higher state of consciousness than you are. It was in reference to this type of mistaken assumption that the scriptures caution a g a i n s t communicating frivolously with beings from other realms and dimensions. Many religions and churches have interpreted this to mean that one should refrain from all forms of channeling. This is definitely not the case. But it most certainly means that you must exercise great discernment. Remember, 'by their fruits you will know them.' Do not blindly accept everything that you or someone else might receive in channeling.

"Before we move on to other matters, I wish to point out to you that all of the great scriptures in Earth are themselves channeled communications. Hence, it is absurd for churches and religions to forbid their followers to communicate with beings from beyond the Earth, when the very teachings upon which all religions are based, have been received in this manner.

"Now let us move on to other matters, Joseph. I want to give you an insight into why previous attempts at finding the actual treasure of El Dorado have failed."

"I, too, am most anxious to learn the answer to that

question, El Dorado, but before you tell me, would you please answer two other questions for me?"

"What are your questions, Joseph?"

"First, in your discourse on channeling, I got the distinct impression that nothing is brought into Earth except through channeling; and that all channeling is a communication with entities beyond the physical realm. Is this a correct impression?"

"The statement itself is correct, Joseph. However, the conclusions that you would draw from this statement, based upon your present knowledge, would be very misleading. In a later discourse we will explore the various aspects of one's own total being and this will clarify your understanding. What is your second question?"

"Why have I been chosen to be entrusted with your great treasure, El Dorado?"

"You have been chosen because of a unique combination of prerequisites and predispositions which you alone upon Earth possess at this given moment. Before you can be entrusted with this vast wealth, however, it must be determined if your predispositions can fulfill the promise of your prerequisites."

"I'm afraid that I do not quite comprehend your answer. Is there any way that you can clarify this for me?"

"Before you were born upon Earth in your present body and personality, Joseph, you had progressed very far in your evolution as a human soul. We are only concerned for the moment with your development as it relates to the planet Earth, and not as it might relate to any other planets, planes or dimensions. Concerning planet Earth, you possess certain prerequisites relating to Earth history that have prepared you for a unique role in this lifetime. Do you understand so far?"

"I believe that I do understand what you are saying, El Dorado. You are saying that I have lived upon the Earth before, and that I have also lived elsewhere. You are therefore talking about reincarnation and I don't believe in the theory of reincarnation. Therefore, how can I believe anything else that you are saying!"

"Remember what I told you a little while ago about keeping an open mind, Joseph? The mere fact that you

cannot accept something at this moment because it conflicts with your past learning experience, don't make the
mistake of rejecting it. Simply set it aside for a time.
Later, when I have finished telling you the whole story,
you will still be free to reject all or part of what I have
told you. Isn't that fair enough?"

"Yes, I suppose so."

"Remember also, when I told you a moment ago that
you possess certain predispositions?"

"Yes."

"Well, these predispositions assure me that you will
not close your mind entirely before you listen at least a
little longer. You see, you have a predisposition for fairness and a predisposition for sensing truths that lie beyond the physical senses. Therefore at this moment you
sense that I will not, and indeed cannot, harm you. I
therefore call upon you to display your predisposition to
fairness and to rely upon your predisposition to sense
truth and listen to me a while longer. Will you do so?"

"Yes. But only so long as I feel that you are not trying to trick me."

"Good! I was certain that you had not closed the
doorway to learning."

"What is the doorway to learning?"

"It is the conscious and subconscious minds."

"How is the doorway closed?

"It is closed by what one has already learned. If this
statement seems paradoxical, let us explore it a bit. Let
us think of something that someone may have learned
in childhood that may have closed their mind for a time,
but which later circumstances forced open. Let's take
the story of the stork that delivers babies from heaven.
This fairy tale seems innocent and innocuous enough for
little children. But is it? Upon close examination we may
find that much harm can be wrought upon the little ones
who so trustingly accept this version of where babies
come from told by their loving and well-meaning parents."

"How?"

"In the first place, the story is a lie. In the second
place, the truth of the beauty and mystery of birth is
obscured to the extent that the fantasy of the stork is
embellished. In the third place, it involves a deception

by someone that we love and trust, thus undermining future trust. In the fourth place, it implants in the subconscious mind erroneous information that must eventually be corrected. In the fifth place, this misinformation provides a false foundation upon which many future thoughts, decisions and choices are based. In the sixth place, until the false information is recognized and weeded out, it obstructs the input of truth. Many other harmful by-products are involved, but the most damaging consequence is the closed mind that can result from having received, accepted and stored false information. This tends to block out receptivity to the truth when it is later received. Also not to be overlooked, is the hurt and pain that is caused when you awaken to the fact that you have been deceived by someone you trusted.

"Unlearning hurts! The more your life has been built on error and misinformation, the greater the pain of unlearning when truth is presented.

"The same observation that we made about the stork can be made with many of the world's religious precepts, many scientific 'facts', many traditions and customs, with just about anything and everything.

"The truth is that so much of what man of Earth has learned about everything is erroneous that it is folly to continue accepting everything at face value. You must learn to discern and discriminate in an enlightened way all information that comes to your attention, before you file it in the computer of your subconscious mind.

"You yourself, Joseph, have undergone some very traumatic unlearning experiences in recent years, so I think that you can appreciate the utter truth of what I have just said."

"Yes. You are so right, El Dorado. I see your point and I certainly agree with you."

"Now, Joseph, I think we can explore together some of the reasons why the treasure of El Dorado has never been discovered."

CHAPTER 2

The Treasure

WHY THE TREASURE
HAS NEVER BEEN DISCOVERED

"As El Dorado, it has been my duty, my role and my privilege to protect this priceless treasure throughout thousands of years of Earth history. You will learn as we proceed that there have been many great civilizations upon Earth that pre-date your recorded history. Each time that man's evolution upon Earth has reached a point where he could advance to a much higher level, this treasure has been made available to a worthy custodian to use for the benefit of all mankind. This has not taken place since the fall of Atlantis 26,000 years ago.

"In recent history, there have been a number of individuals who have sought unsuccessfully to uncover this vast wealth. However, it is so well guarded that accidental discovery is impossible. The reason for this is obvious. Were this wealth to fall into the wrong hands, it could literally destroy mankind. Furthermore, before this vast wealth can even be entrusted to the proper custodian, he must be carefully and thoroughly groomed and prepared through a series of lifetimes. Finally, in the lifetime during which the custodian assumes control of the treasure, he must go through an arduous cleansing process. This process is designed to totally cleanse, purify and awaken the physical, mental, emotional and soul (subconscious) aspects. In addition, the custodian must be brought to a point of awareness where he understands and appreciates that there is a Divine Plan unfolding upon Earth. He must also understand and appreciate the interplay that is occuring between Earth and other planets, planes and dimensions. *For it is only by understanding this that he can properly cooperate with entities beyond Earth and coordinate the use of the treasure for the proper benefit of mankind.* Is this explanation meaningful to you?"

"Yes, I must admit that it does sound perfectly meaningful to me. Perhaps it is because I want to believe it. Perhaps it is because since my early childhood I have dreamed of amassing great wealth to use for bettering conditions upon the Earth, for educating mankind and for alleviating suffering brought about by ignorance and lack of opportunity.

"Your statement about being prepared for many lifetimes disturbs me though, because it begs the theory of reincarnation. However, if reincarnation really IS a fact of universal life, perhaps that would explain my preoccupation with the idea of great wealth and service to mankind all of my life. In any event, I will keep an open mind. I can see from what you have already said about the cleansing process that much has already taken place with me in this lifetime. I have really been put through the wringer in unlearning a lot of false ideas!"

"And you still have a long way to go, Joseph."

"The fact that I have come this far gives me the courage that I need to go farther."

"You must be able to demonstrate self-mastery, Joseph. In order to do this you must know yourself. In order to know yourself you must be able to explore every facet of your being. In order to explore every facet of your being, you must first be aware of the existence of these various facets. I will aid you in this. So now, we arrive at the beginning. And the beginning, as I have said, is to 'know thyself.' The central theme of three of Earth's greatest teachers has revolved around the admonition 'know thyself.' These teachers were Gautama the Buddha, Socrates and Jesus the Christ of Nazareth. So we have it on good authority, don't we?"

"On very good authority, I would say. I have the utmost respect for all three of these great men. But getting back to the treasure for a moment, is it your intention to actually place this whole vast treasure of El Dorado in my hands?"

"It is, providing you prepare yourself properly."

"I certainly intend to do all that I can to adequately prepare myself. If you will pardon my curiosity for a moment, can you give me any idea of the actual value of your treasure, measured in dollars?"

"You must bear in mind, Joseph, that much of the treasure is beyond such measurement, for it consists of concepts, inventions, technologies, knowledge, in addition to the vast tangible treasure of precious metals and minerals, artifacts of past civilizations and secret locations of unmined natural resources. The most valuable asset of the treasure is literally priceless, since it could

44

not be purchased with all of the material wealth of all the worlds. The asset to which I refer is the secret of overcoming death and transmuting oneself into the cosmic consciousness of the fourth dimensional 'light' body.

"However, if one were to attempt to place any such dollar value on this treasure, one would certainly have to think in terms of hundreds of billions of dollars."

"Hundreds of billions of dollars? That is an absolutely staggering amount!"

"Does it frighten you?"

"It most certainly awes me!"

"It would awe anyone. In a way, it even awes me, and I dwell in the etheric (Christ) realms of our solar system where one is not easily awed by anything on the physical planes of expression! It is well for you to contemplate the size and value of this great treasure. The more you contemplate, the more you will work to prepare yourself for assuming this awesome responsibility."

"I'm beginning to realize more and more that I have a long way to go to be fully prepared."

"Yes, you have a long way to go, but you don't have a long time to accomplish your preparation. Due to the fact that much of your preparation was accomplished in past lives, however, we can greatly accelerate your learning process in this life. Come, let us begin."

"I'm ready!"

"Say the Lord's Prayer in the manner that I have taught you."

"I say it frequently."

"This time think it as you're saying it. Don't think about any religious context in connection with it. Think only in terms of Universal Law. The Lord's Prayer is perhaps the most concise, comprehensive and effective formula in Earth to achieve a balanced state of being, and to cleanse oneself of hatred and negativity, if it is said with full sincerity and comprehension."

"Our Father
Which art in heaven
Hallowed be Thy name
Thy kingdom come

Thy will be done

In Earth, as it is in heaven

Give us this day our daily bread

And forgive us our debts as we have forgiven our
   debtors (long pause)

You leave us not in temptation

You will deliver us from evil

For Thine is the kingdom

Thine is the power

Thine is the glory, forever. Amen."

"Good, Joseph. I noticed when you said 'and forgive
us our debts as we have forgiven our debtors', that you
paused a long time in thoughtful meditation."

"Yes. I think that perhaps this is the first time in
my life that I really and fully comprehended the meaning
of this statement, this law. As a consequence of this
insight, I suddenly feel very different, very elated."

"I am elated along with you. I can read your mind,
and I know that you have just experienced the most important realization of your lifetime. Would you like to
express your feelings aloud in words?"

"Yes, I would. I know it's the most important thing
that has ever happened to me and I want to reinforce
and crystalize this beautiful moment by telling you of the
immensity of this realization. I am so overjoyed that I
may have difficulty collecting my thoughts and expressing them. I realized for the first time that the forgiveness
which we ask for ourselves is conditional to the forgiveness we render to our fellow man in our own hearts. When
I realized this, I simultaneously realized that I had never
really forgiven many offenses that others have com-
mitted against me. For a moment I was appalled. I
thought of my audacity in asking forgiveness for my
own numerous and grievous offenses against my fellow
man and against God, when in reality I was unforgiving
in my own heart. When the horrible duplicity and hypoc-
risy of this hit me, I was dumbstruck and filled with
shame and remorse. I immediately said a silent prayer of
forgiveness in my heart, releasing all debts that I felt
anyone owed me in this life. As I did so, my whole being
was flooded with light and ecstasy, and I realized that I
had rid myself of a tremendous burden. At that moment

46

I was literally overflowing with pure joy. While digesting the immensity of this event, another thought came to me. I thought, what if reincarnation were a fact, a reality of the Universe? What if I have had a number of past lives? What if unforgiving thoughts from those past lives were still lodged within my soul? What a horrible thought! I resolved that if this were so, then I must forgive everyone for everything done against me in any past lifetime, no matter how heinous the offense. I performed another act of forgiveness. I was again flooded with light, more brilliant and intense than the first. This time I heard the most beautiful and melodious music and saw the most vibrant and thrilling colors I have ever seen. I heard a choir of thousands of angelic beings singing thanks for the release from this negativity that had bound me for who knows how long. It was as if a tremendous weight had been suddenly lifted from me, and simultaneously I felt myself rising through space accompanied by countless heavenly beings who were all smiles, all happiness, all loving. I just cannot begin to express this moment—this event, in words. It surely is the most important happening of my life!"

"It surely is, Joseph. And the beginning of a new life."

"I feel a bit strange resuming our discussion on a mundane level, El Dorado, but can you tell me some of the other reasons why your treasure has never been discovered?"

"As we have already seen, the treasure can only be 'discovered' by its proper custodian. And, of course, the custodian must be fully prepared before that event can come about. Also, man's development must reach an acceptable level in order to be able to use the treasure. It is only now that these conditions are being met.

"In preparation for this 20th century happening, you had an incarnation in the 14th century in South America as an Indian chief. It was the purpose of that lifetime to establish a modern legend of El Dorado upon Earth."

"Yes; I have heard of the legend of El Dorado."

"What do you remember about it?"

"Well, basically, I remember that a tribe of Indians existed, the Chibchas, who lived in what is now Colombia, in the tableland of Bogota on Lake Guatavita. Their king or chief was known as the 'golden one' or the 'gilded man'. He received this name from a strange ceremony they observed in investing a new chief. When a new chief was chosen, the priests and elders would bear him to Lake Guatavita on a litter adorned with gold. The body of the new chief was anointed with a sticky substance and then covered with gleaming gold dust. He was then rowed out onto the lake on an elaborate raft that was loaded with gold and jeweled treasures. The chief then dove into the lake to wash the gold dust from his body while the gold and jewels were being thrown into the lake as offerings.

"When the Spaniards heard of this custom they named the chief El Dorado, which means the 'gilded one' or the 'golden one'. As the story spread, El Dorado became a legendary priest-king who ruled over a kingdom of mysterious people in South America whose cities were paved and palaced in solid gold. It was only natural that such a legend would stimulate a great quest for this treasure."

"You seem to remember a lot about this legend, Joseph."

"I must admit that it has always fascinated me. In fact, I have always been attracted to Colombia, and have thought of hunting there for gold and emeralds. I have even dreamed of it several times. I am walking through a jungle in this recurring dream, when I discover what appears to be an old ruin. While exploring this ruin, I move a large stone which uncovers a hidden stairway leading downwards to a huge room. Naturally, my curiosity leads me down into this room 20 or 30 feet below the ground. The room itself is about 40 feet wide by 60 or 70 feet long. The ceiling is 12 to 14 feet high, perhaps a bit higher. I am always fascinated when I enter this room. It is a study in contrasts. The floor, walls and ceiling are all smooth. It consists of a dense, glass-like rock with a mirror smooth finish. It appears to be polished obsidian. There are a lot of gold objects on the walls and tables all around the room. On the wall opposite the entrance, there is a huge gold medallion or shield that must be at least 10 feet in diameter. This medallion is the focal point of the whole room. The room is filled with the most intensely fascinating, precious objects, each one more distracting and compelling than the other, yet they all fade in comparison to that magnificent medallion. There seems to be no light source within the room, yet the room is well lit and everything in the room can be seen clearly. In fact, you could say that everything stands out sharply. But the gold medallion seems to be bathed in a special light all its own. It draws me hypnotically each time I have the dream. I can see clearly even across the full length of the room how the medallion is embossed and chased. It is as if the medallion were speaking to me and it were saying, 'You can read me. I have a very interesting story to tell you. Just study me and I will reveal to you all of the riches of the Earth'. Then as I approach it, I am overcome with the feeling that I could walk right into this great medallion and become part of it. When I stand at the base of it, I know that I am looking at the history of planet Earth and I know how to read and interpret it. I realize, too, that the treasures in this great room are but a small representation of what lies hidden in various other parts of Earth, and that the secret locations of Earth's great treasures are all encoded in some way in the great medallion! And I have the feeling in my dream that I am the only one in Earth at the moment who can decipher the code! This dream always feels so real that I could swear that I am really there—that it is really taking place.

"It is no dream, Joseph!"

"What!"

"I know that you are familiar with astral travel from your study of psychic phenomena."

"Yes."

"What you have failed to understand and appreciate is that you have made many such astral journeys while you were resting your physical body in the sleep state. In this instance, as in many other instances, it is I who have repeatedly taken you on this particular journey to familiarize you with an event that is soon to take place in your waking life! The room is real. It really does exist. It is one of many such rooms in various parts of Earth. You have described it quite well. The great medallion itself consists of several thousand pounds of pure 24 carat gold which has been etherically energized to receive and project thought impressions. Its metallic value on today's gold market would be millions of dollars. However, as you know, the information it contains is literally priceless. It is a focal point for higher energies, and therein lies its intrinsic value."

"This is an extraordinary revelation, El Dorado! I get goose bumps just thinking about it, because I know what you're saying is true. My God, what a feeling!"

"Let me give you an example, Joseph, of the unique powers and energies surrounding the secret room. Do you recall from your reading of the legend of El Dorado, a Spaniard named Gonzalo Jimenez de Quesada, who led an expedition in search of El Dorado?"

"Yes. I remember reading that he actually found a lot of gold and emeralds. I should say he plundered them. But he never found the city that was paved with gold. I also remember reading about Sir Walter Raleigh and someone else, I think named Orellana, and also a brother of Pizarro, among others, who sought the treasure unsuccessfully."

"Well it was Jimenez de Quesada who passed directly over the secret room. Actually, he stopped directly above the room, for he was gripped with a sudden curiosity about the ruins. While he paused within the force field, he suddenly felt tremendously repulsed by the place. The repulsion might accurately be compared to two north poles of a magnet side by side. They cannot remain in position, as you know, because a powerful force repels each from the other. All of Earth's secret rooms are similarly protected by a powerful force field that keeps anyone from discovering any of them. Of course, if someone of great power and knowledge did overcome the repulsion of the force field, other sources would intervene to safeguard the treasures. Jimenez de Quesada's curiosity about the ruins was shortlived because of the extreme discomfort that he associated with the ruins. Once this feeling possessed him, he couldn't leave fast enough.

"The most obvious example of the effectiveness of the safeguards protecting Earth's secret records rooms is the continuing inviolability of the secret room in the Great Pyramid of Giza. For literally centuries, man has been trying to locate Giza's secret room, often employing the most sophisticated scientific techniques and instruments which Earth has to offer. To no avail. No Earthly power will reveal these secrets. These sacred records are being protected by a higher power until the proper time for their revelation.

"Since your preparation as Custodian of this treasure involves extensive further growth, and time is short let us move on to other matters."

CHAPTER 3

An Open Mind Exercise

"Have you ever thought of the planet Earth as a living being, Joseph; a living entity in its own right with its own consciousness, its own mind, its own development potential?"

"No, I can't say that I have ever given that concept any consideration, El Dorado. What is the purpose of the question?"

"This question has the same purpose as all of my questions — to open your mind to new ideas — and help develop the capabilities of your mind—to literally force it to expand and condition you to face concepts with which you are totally unfamiliar in this life and think your way through them to a conclusion. You see, a wealth of knowledge is hidden in your subconscious mind. Unfortunately, it will stay hidden there unless positive action is taken to pull it out from its hiding place. The subconscious mind does not yield its treasures to an undeserving consciousness any more than the Treasure of El Dorado is given to an unworthy custodian. So, from this point onward you may confidently expect your mind to be stretched to the limit of its pliability. In this manner you will grow rapidly in wisdom, knowledge and understanding. I am now going to leave you for a day. When I return tomorrow, you will tell me about the possibilities of planets as living beings. You are not to consult any books. You are not to seek the opinions of others. What you tell me when I return is to be the product of your own conscious and subconscious minds, combined with your intuition, inspiration and imagination. As further training in the faculty of expression and mental discipline, you are to express yourself in the most succinct manner possible. Are these instructions clear to you?"

"Yes."

"Good. I will communicate with you in 24 hours."

24 HOURS LATER

"Joseph, this is El Dorado."

"I know. Your presence brings a vibrancy to me that is beyond explaining. I'm glad you're back."

"I understand what you mean. Are you prepared, Joseph?"

"I have given the possibility of planets as living beings as much thought as possible in so short a time. Whether or not I am prepared is for you to judge.

"After your challenge yesterday, I decided that the best approach to take would be to assume that planets are living beings. By looking at them in this way I could then project myself into the role of a planetary being and begin looking at my own body and mind and environment. Frankly, some of my thoughts have astounded me.

"The first thing that occurred to me was the teeming abundance of life and movement that was taking place upon my 'skin' and within my body. I thought of the constant motion and movement of the oceans and rivers and winds and I realized that I would be able to feel them. I then thought of the constant motion and movement of the various life forces upon my 'skin' and realized that I could not feel them. I thought of the billions of human beings and animals and countless lesser creatures, and knew that I probably could not see them and might not even be aware of their presence except from the results they produced. At the same time, I realized that their presence could greatly affect my health and well-being. I thought of the analogy of countless bacteria that live on and in the human body and greatly affect the welfare of that body. The bacteria on humans can be friendly or un-friendly, helpful or harmful. The same could easily be said of the life forms living on my Earth skin.

"I thought of the pollution mankind has created and its effects upon my well-being. I thought of mental and emotional as well as purely physical pollution. I could readily sense the pain and discomfort of a nuclear explosion occurring on or beneath my 'skin'. I could feel my anxiety at having my vision of the visible universe obscured by a growing cloud of pollution befouling the atmosphere around me.

"I wondered if this misuse of my body by its inhabitants could be the cause of certain illnesses or upheavals that I occasionally suffered such as earthquakes (virus-like convulsions caused by humans), volcanoes (boil-like eruptions produced by the discharge of poisons), hurricanes, typhoons and the like (colds and respiratory diseases induced by imbalance caused by pollution). I couldn't help but wonder if the occasional shifting of the polar axis might not be the end result of an overaccumulation of negative thought forms produced by centuries of negligence and ignorance by the unfriendly parasites living on my surface! Then I thought of heat waves (fever), cold waves (chills) induced by my proximity to the sun.

"Next, my mind wandered to underground rivers and reservoirs of oil, and I could compare these to blood vessels and arteries. When I thought of vast concentrations of metals and minerals I thought of glands and nerves. I considered the inner heat that might exist at my core and wondered if this was the divine life force existing within all living beings. I quickly rejected this idea when I considered that the life force is less physical in nature and it is the divine life force which gives life to the physical as I will show later.

"When I considered the magnetic pole, it occurred to me that the brain activity of human beings creates a similar force field in the body. Perhaps then the magnetic pole represented the focal point of my mind as a planet.

"Of course I could not escape comparing the Earth and its fellow planets orbiting the sun to the electrons in orbit around the proton neutron mass of an atom. Would this be another example of the macro-micro unity in the universe? This thought made me realize that there is nothing motionless or stagnant in the universe. From the smallest unit of which we are aware to the largest heavenly bodies, there is constant motion and life.

"My mind drifted back to the underground rivers coursing beneath my skin and I became aware of the vital effect that this could have upon the activity of creatures living upon my surface. The movement of this underground water would produce an easily measurable force field of electrical energy which could be beneficial and useful to those creatures if they knew of its existence and could learn how to use it. I knew that this flow of electrical energy could be tapped and used to replace present energy sources at negligible cost. I realized that energy itself was limitless throughout the universe and that the thought of an energy crisis was absurd. Man has only to release his imagination from the confining strictures of conventional thinking, and the whole universe will beckon to him and yield its wonders beyond belief!

"Upon coming to this realization, I began to give freer reign to my thought flow. At this point it made no difference whether my thoughts were the product of imagination, inspiration or intuition. What did matter was that I instinctively recognized far-reaching possibilities in the principles that were springing forth from my mind. So if I stray a bit from the specific subject of considering the planet Earth as a living being, it will be in the interest of sharing what is to me a new-found capacity for creative reasoning. I promise to be succinct."

"I approve of your progress thus far, Joseph. Please continue."

"I could not release the thought of limitless energy available everywhere throughout the universe. Perhaps it was the irony of what was happening to my surface today in the 'energy crisis' that mankind was suffering. How could there be an energy crisis in the presence of literally limitless energy forces? I began thinking of where man's quest for new energy sources had led him. The following came readily to my mind: the harnessing of the momentum of moving waters, converting the movements of air, using fossil fuels and nuclear reactors as a heat source to produce steam from water to propel generators, burning refined fossil fuels in engines which run generators, catalytic chemical conversion, solar cells, etc.

"As I was pondering these known sources of energy, my intuition told me that an individual in the United States had come across a method of converting energy into usable form through a liquid metal fast breeder reactor! My intuition further told me that this process would produce electric current cheaply and abundantly *for the masses*, thereby freeing mankind from the dependency and the exploitation of oil producing countries. Furthermore, it would help preserve my natural resources for future generations. The significance of this discovery would burst upon a startled world with profound effect! Selfish vested interests would be caught unprepared! Cartels would collapse! Mankind would benefit!

"Later, someone would learn how to tap the awesome energy that surrounds my surface in the form of day and night or light and dark forces. Once this interaction of light and dark was understood, then man would have arrived at one of the ultimate energy sources. At all times my surface was divided between lightness and darkness and at all times the areas covered by light and dark were changing. I could envision a worldlike connecting device linked around my solar middle (the belt of greatest sun exposure) that could in some way produce energy through the interplay of light and dark forces. In the same manner, I could envision a worldwide connecting device linking the polar regions with the tropic and subtropic regions and producing energy through an interplay of hot and cold forces.

"My last energy producing theory was the most exotic. It would surely be totally rejected by the scientific community."

"That is reason enough to give it serious study. Let me hear it."

"Everyone and everything has its counterpart in spirit, whether it is man or animal, plant or mineral, or the smallest or largest composite thing such as an atom or a planet or a star. In man and animal, plant and mineral we call it an aura. Kirlian photography is now revealing to scientists and skeptics alike what clairvoyants have long known about the reality of this force field. It is electrical in nature as is everything in the universe and it exists independently of the object that it surrounds and permeates. It is, in fact, the viable form which continues to function when the physical life form dies. Scientists have already demonstrated that when a human being 'dies', the physical body becomes measurably lighter. The reason for this is that the 'spirit' part of our being takes leave of the mortal body which is no longer functioning. What most people fail to understand is that the 'spirit' counterpart has substance. The reason that it is not readily seen by most people is that its range of vibration renders it invisible to the physical eye. It can be seen clairvoyantly by those whose spiritual faculties are highly developed. One's consciousness and other higher faculties reside in this 'spiritual' body, and are indestructible. This accounts for the many cases when people have 'died' on the operating table and later been brought back to 'life', relating how they viewed the whole incident from outside of their body and later rejoined their body.

"Now my point is this. The Earth is a living being. As a living being, it has its own aura or 'spiritual' body which surrounds and permeates it. This aura has form and substance and exists independently of the physical vibration of the planet. Perhaps the so-called Van Allen radiation belt that encircles the Earth from a distance of from 300 to 4,000 or so miles, is in reality the Earth's auric force field, and represents the 'spiritual' body of the planet Earth. Just as the opposites of light and dark, hot and cold, produce an electrical energy flow, I am convinced that the opposites of physical and spiritual somehow do the same.

"I would like to add just a few more thoughts while I'm on the subject. This auric or spiritual world that surrounds and permeates the physical Earth, must be the abode of many people when they pass out of their physical bodies. I don't mean to imply by any means that it is the dwelling place for all, but I can certainly see it as a dwelling place for many who are not aware of the worlds that exist beyond that.

"The last thoughts of any consequence that I had on the subject concerned the sun and planets as well as the other solar systems, galaxies and universes. I realized that if I, a planet, were possessed of a life force consisting of intelligence, awareness, vitality and therefore immortality as an individualized consciousness, then naturally my fellow planets and stars were likewise living beings, the same as I. This thought in turn initiated a whole series of thoughts concerning the interactions of planetary forces, communication among these intelligences, whether or not whole universes were still greater beings comprising many galaxies, etc. Given another 24 hours, I feel that I could have developed some exciting possibilities along this line of thinking."

"You have shown much independence of thought, Joseph. Considering that I gave you only 24 hours to prepare, you have done well. This was a lesson in which you had an opportunity to demonstrate open-mindedness to yourself. You passed the test, because it is obvious that you did not permit your preconceptions to dominate. Had you done so, it would have inhibited the freedom and latitude that you expressed. Tell me, what did you conclude regarding the concept of Earth as a living being?"

"As surprising as it seems to me to say this, I have concluded that the Earth is indeed a living being! Of

course I cannot prove it, but I now 'feel' it very strongly
—intuitively."

"You are correct."

"Two weeks ago I wouldn't have considered making such a statement."

"You are not the same man you were two weeks ago, Joseph. Two weeks hence you will not be the same that you are now.

"To further stimulate your progress at this time, I am going to fulfill a promise that I made you at the beginning. You will recall I told you that I would introduce you to other masters from time to time, who would speak to you about subjects of great importance. Tomorrow, one of the great master teachers of our solar system will accompany me. He will speak to you about the Divine Plan that is unfolding upon Earth, and also about the reality of the Universal Law of reincarnation. You will be quite amazed at what he has to say. I will not spoil the surprise in store for you by telling you any more. I will see you tomorrow."

CHAPTER 4

The Divine Plan Unfolds

Sananda Tells Of The Many
Lives Of Jesus

"Greetings, Joseph!"

"Hello, El Dorado. I have been anxiously awaiting your return as well as the privilege of meeting the great master teacher that you said would be accompanying you today."

"Your waiting will be amply rewarded, Joseph, when you learn the identity of my friend. I will not keep you in suspense, but will immediately remove my vibration from your aura so that our 'guest speaker' may begin his discourse."

As El Dorado left my auric field, I could feel the presence of the other master as he entered it. It is impossible to describe the ecstatic feelings and sensations I experienced when this great master entered into my aura. He began to communicate with me in a very simple, straightforward manner as follows:

"My beloved Joseph, El Dorado has been keeping me informed of your rapid progress. We are all very pleased with your attitude and with your spirit of dedication. We rely greatly upon you, and thousands like you, to help bring mankind up out of the darkness of his subconscious prison into the light of his superconscious inspiration. Please listen carefully to my little story and record it faithfully.

A Divine Plan is unfolding upon Earth. The majority of those incarnated on the planet cannot see or sense this plan. They're too involved in more important things— like earning a living, going to school, raising children, supporting families, fighting for causes, or perhaps just enjoying the fruits of Earth. There is no end to the concerns that are more urgent and more important than seeing or sensing this marvelous plan that is transmuting our planet and everything upon it.

"Let me tell you of what it reminds me. Can you imagine a giant ocean liner in the middle of the ocean with thousands of passengers on board? Now just imagine that most of these passengers do not remember who they are or where they came from. Also, they do not know their port of destination. Almost everyone you ask has a different concept of how they got aboard the ship because they cannot remember coming aboard. Never having seen another ship or aircraft or a landfall, they believe that they are the only human beings anywhere.

"At this point, let's perform a little sleight of mind. Let's change this ocean liner into Spaceship Earth and visualize similar circumstances. This should not be too difficult because most people do not remember coming aboard Earth. Truly, most people do not remember who they are. They identify totally with their mortal personality. They give scant thought to the possibility of having lived before in another body on Earth or elsewhere. They have probably given no thought to the possibility of having lived as a spiritual being in another dimension. Likewise, most people do not give much thought to the possibility of human life outside Earth. And it is a certainty that most people do not realize their destination when they die a physical death.

"Well let's get back to the ship, Joseph. The ship has a captain and a crew. Surely the captain knows the destination of his ship, and some of the crew are aware of it, since the captain does not sail the ship alone. Just as a ship must have a captain and crew, so our Spaceship Earth must in its journey through space, time and dimensions, have a captain and crew who are responsible for bringing mankind on Earth to its proper destination or destiny in conformity with the Divine Plan. Thus, it is obvious that there are those who have some of the answers and who know the itinerary.

"I am the spiritual captain of Spaceship Earth, Joseph. I am known throughout the Solar System and beyond as Sananda. The crew of Spaceship Earth is that faithful band of 'light workers' who assist in implementing the Divine Plan—who work in the light, and for the enlightenment of mankind.

"In my role as spiritual leader, I have had many incarnations upon Earth. At each incarnation in that capacity I brought forth the information and enlightenment which a particular segment of mankind needed at that time to advance it in understanding and growth.

"For example, one of my incarnations was as Moses. In that lifetime, my purpose was to bring forth the spiritual laws which the people of that era could understand and accept, and also to lead the children of Israel out of the bondage of Egypt into the promised land. In accomplishing this, I was also fulfilling a previous prophecy.

"A later incarnation was as Elisha (Eliseus), the

servant of Elias (Elijah), and his successor in the prophetic ministry. Many have since been led to see in Elisha an incarnation of the Christ. Elisha has often been referred to as a forerunner of Jesus. As did Elias, I, as Elisha defended the revealed laws against paganism, worked 'miracles' and prophesied.

"In my lifetime as Jesus the Christ of Nazareth, I came to fulfill the law (Moses), and the prophets (Elisha), and to show by the example of my life a new level of consciousness, the cosmic christ consciousness. My life as Jesus was the culmination of all of my previous Earth incarnations. In this incarnation, I taught and exemplified the great secrets of the ages. The sense and reality of these teachings have been little understood up to this point. Only now, after almost 2,000 years, are a few pockets of comprehension and understanding beginning to appear. All of my teachings centered upon one crucial goal for man of Earth—that he become aware of the meaning of cosmic (christ) consciousness, and that he desire to attain this level of manifestation and development!

"Let us dwell for a moment upon some vitally significant correlations in my three lives as Moses, Elisha and Jesus of Nazareth. We see reflected in these three incarnations an *intelligent plan* and pattern to benefit the children of Israel, and concurrently, all of mankind. As Moses, I brought forth the law and led the Israelites from bondage to where they would be free to practice these revealed laws. As Elisha, I came to defend the revealed laws against the threats of paganism, and to prophesy. As Jesus, I came to fulfill both the law and the prophets.

"As the Divine Plan has unfolded throughout the centuries, many members of the spiritual family of 'light workers' have been simultaneously incarnated to work together and bring about various aspects of the Plan. A typical example of this teamwork was the incarnation of Elias (Elijah) and also that of John the Baptist, who were one and the same entity (see Matt. 11:13-15 and 17:11-13). In the incarnations of Elisha-Jesus it was the mission of Elias-John to prepare the way, to be the forerunner, the harbinger.

"That this plan was and is being actively aided and implemented from beyond Earth has been amply demonstrated by extraterrestrial occurrences in my lives as

Moses, Elisha and Jesus. This is revealed in the following happenings, or 'miracles', which are recorded in the Scriptures, but which were not understood at that time (or apparently since) : when 'God' appeared to Moses in a burning bush, when the Red Sea parted, when Moses received the Tablets at Sinai, when Elias was taken up by a 'whirlwind' (a fiery chariot) into 'heaven', when the waters of the Jordan were parted, when the 'star' led the three Wise Men to Bethlehem at the time of the birth of Jesus, etc. In capsulizing the unfolding Plan, Joseph, I can not emphasize too strongly the importance of the assistance being rendered to the 'light workers' upon Earth by our brothers from other planets and dimensions. Throughout recorded history, in many scriptures and legends, there are references to spacecraft and extraterrestrial beings appearing to men of Earth. They are appearing today in ever greater numbers all over Earth, as part of an intelligent, coordinated, Divine Plan that affects the entire Solar System and beyond.

"Before mentioning other pertinent Earth incarnations of mine, I want to emphasize the importance of that faithful group of 'light workers'. Little could have been accomplished if I had worked alone. Therefore, before, during and after each lifetime when I have had an Earthly incarnation, a large number of 'light workers' were incarnated to assist in many ways. One of these workers, Elias-John the Baptist, has already been mentioned. Later, I will give you some other specific examples of incarnated members of the Spiritual Hierarchy working together.

"Let us now look at my incarnations between my life as Moses and my life as Jesus of Nazareth. You see, Joseph, in my role as spiritual leader of Earth, I have been concerned with the growth and understanding of all men of Earth, not only the Israelites.

"Following the lifetime of Elisha, I was reincarnated as Zoroaster (Zarathustra) in northern Persia, between the 7th and 6th centuries B.C. The Persian empire at that time was much vaster than present day Persia (Iran). It extended from Northeast Africa and what is now Turkey on the West, to the Indus River on the East. It included much of Earth's population that lacked formalized spiritual teachings to raise man's consciousness. To this

68

land that bridged the Occidental and the Oriental cultures, Zoroaster brought the ethical teachings of righteousness, immortality, good thought, perfect health, dominion and the beauty of holiness.

"About 563 B. C., I again took on Earthly flesh in the person of Siddhartha Gautama. This was certainly an important lifetime. At one time, probably a third or more of the people in Earth were followers of the Buddha. It is easy to see the pattern and *the Plan* that was unfolding to raise the consciousness of mankind. In the course of a few centuries, we can trace my influence as spiritual ruler of this planet from Moses, the lawgiver of the Israelites, through the prophet Elisha of the Israelites, through the Persian poet, religious teacher-philosopher, Zoroaster, to the Buddha, who brought enlightenment to the Eastern world. I was able to bridge the gulf between Occidental and Oriental by providing each with the kind of teaching of the *same truths* which could be accepted by their widely differing cultures.

"However—this still left an important part of the 'civilized' world without ethical truths to advance its understanding. Into this moral vacuum, I was incarnated as Socrates to teach the people to 'know thyself'. As you will recall, Joseph, Socrates believed that the goodness in man was based on wisdom and that wickedness was based on ignorance.

"With these lifetimes, I succeeded in bringing forth something for everyone, whether Israelite, Occidental, Oriental or Pagan. It is important to discover the common thread woven throughout all of my teachings, 'know thyself'!

"Is it possible, Joseph, to view these lives in the light in which they are presented, and miss seeing part of the Divine Plan that has been unfolding upon Earth for men to grasp?"

"This is an amazing revelation, Sananda. I, like most other people, have never even considered the possibility that one leader, one teacher might have brought forth these spiritual truths. When one does not believe in reincarnation, such a thought isn't even possible to begin with. In the light of what you have presented, however, I can indeed begin to see a Divine Plan unfolding."

"How do you think this might affect your concepts concerning religions?"

"The most obvious effect is the irony that one being, one person, in the guise of different lifetimes and different personalities, could in fact, be the avatar whose teachings founded many different world religions. A further irony lies in the fact that these teachings were probably never intended to be a foundation upon which to build an institutional church, but were intended instead to introduce mankind to the progressive flow of higher truths leading him into a higher state of consciousness. A still greater irony lies in the fact that each of these religions has opposed each of the others over the centuries. I would say that my greatest realization concerning religions was that the religions of most believing people were counter-productive to the fulfilment of the teachings upon which they were originally based."

"Beautifully spoken, Joseph, and yet sadly true.

"At this point, I want to give you a few further examples of how members of the Spiritual Hierarchy incarnate together to carry out the work of the Divine Plan.

"When I was Socrates, Plato was one of my students who later became one of the most renowned ethical philosophers of Western culture, influencing all subsequent philosophical thought. One of Plato's students was Aristotle, certainly one of the greatest thinkers in Western culture. The positive impact of the lives of both Plato and Aristotle upon the world is a matter of public knowledge throughout civilization. In my incarnation as Jesus of Nazareth, Plato played the role of the Apostle Paul, while Aristotle was my beloved Apostle John. The implications of these roles is obvious to any truth seeker, but will remain somewhat obscure until one reaches the true state of cosmic consciousness. For it is only upon reaching cosmic consciousness that one can truly see all things as they are.

"Before concluding, I would mention my beloved twin soul, Mary, known to you as the mother of Jesus of Nazareth. Mary has served with me in many different relationships, in many different Earth incarnations. For instance, when I was Gautama Siddhartha, before becoming the Buddha, I took a wife called Yasodhara. This

70

was Mary. I tell you these things, Joseph, to stir your soul (subconscious) memories, to help remind you that you, too, play a role in the Divine Plan, as do countless thousands of other 'light workers' in Earth.

"Remember well these things that I have just told you for the time has come to make them known to others.

"Remember, also, that the greatest book in Earth, the Judeo-Christian Scriptures, will soon be interpreted by one of my present incarnates. When this occurs, then will come the great apostasy as prophesied. Little does man of Earth realize at this moment, that the Bible is a scientific treatise on universal nuclear physics, written in a universal metaphysical language which discloses in minute detail, the precise prescription, or formula, for the attainment of cosmic (christ) consciousness. Be very aware of this, Joseph, for as I have said, you have a role to play in this Universal drama.

"I leave you now for a time, but I shall, at the appropriate moment, return to you in yet another guise. I love you, and all of mankind!"

"Goodbye, Sananda. I love you, and I thank you for the enlightenment that you have given me. I look forward to seeing you again soon."

CHAPTER 5

The Unfolding Plan—Part II

Kut Humi Speaks On
Atlantis
and
Human Life On Other Planets

It was two long weeks before El Dorado again made contact with me. During this time I began to wonder if perhaps I had done something wrong that had caused him to desert me. I decided that I had best spend this time studying hard instead of worrying.

I did a lot of reading about the lives of the great avatars, prophets and teachers, searching for the common thread that Sananda had referred to — 'know thyself'. Also, I was trying to identify with various historical figures to see if it would awaken in me any conscious memory of having lived a past lifetime. Nothing happened. Finally, El Dorado appeared.

"Hello Joseph! It is I, El Dorado."

"I know it is you, El Dorado. I can recognize your vibration. I certainly have missed you. It has been a long two weeks without your presence."

"There was no moment during the two weeks when I was not in your presence, Joseph. The mere absence of this type of mental communication is, in itself, no indication that I am gone. Try to be more perceptive. Pay closer attention to the feelings around your solar plexus and your heart area. Also try to be aware of delicate touching sensations about the head and face. Learn to 'feel' with your whole being and to translate these 'feelings' into viable thought patterns. Soon, little will escape your attention.

"Tell me of your progress during my silence."

"I have been studying very hard, trying to free my mind of the inhibiting effects of a lifetime spent within orthodox teachings."

"And what has been the result?"

"As I have progressed in my studies, I have begun to see the wisdom of looking beyond one's own limited viewpoint. I have become painfully aware of the stout walls within which orthodoxy keeps us subtly trapped. Upon realizing this, I cautiously scaled the walls on a ladder of logic and light, and begun to gaze enthralled at the panorama of limitless knowledge and wisdom that lies beyond!"

"I am very pleased with the direction in which you are moving, Joseph. You are beginning to demonstrate some independence of thought which is quite beautiful.

"I have another surprise in store for you. Accompanying me today is the great Master Teacher and Cosmic Christ, Kut Humi. Sananda has already mentioned something about Kut Humi to you in the last discourse. The incarnations of Aristotle and John the Beloved were Earth embodiments of Kut Humi. Other incarnations with which you might be familiar are Elihu (also spelled Eliu —from the Book of Job 32-37), Lao-Tze (also spelled Laotse and LaoTzu, 6th century B. C. in China, upon whose teachings the Taoist religon is based), Theodosius the Great (emperor of Rome, 4th century A. D.), St. Columba (known as the Apostle of Caledonia, helped to convert Scotland to Christianity, 5th century A. D.), St. Francis of Assisi (Italy 12th-13th century A. D., founder of the Francisan Order), Leonardo da Vinci (Italian painter, sculptor, architect, engineer and scientist, 15th-16th century A. D.). A careful study of these life patterns will reveal still further evidence of the Divine Plan manifesting itself through the willing efforts and sacrifices of dedicated beings.

"Kut Humi has come to speak to you on the subject of Atlantis and its relationship to the present. In this connection he will also tell you of coming changes in our solar system and of life on other planets. I now step aside so that the Master Kut Humi can begin your instruction."

As was the case when Sananda entered my auric force field, I was totally infused with an ineffable feeling of ecstasy, love, euphoria and sense of perfect wellbeing, as Kut Humi anchored his vibration within mine. He spoke to me and said:

"What are you feeling, Joseph, is the intensity of the Divine Love vibration that is always manifested in the Christ realms. Later, El Dorado will explain it to you in more scientific terms. For now, I have other vitally important information to impart to you. As you will soon realize, we are bringing you a systematic series of discourses which are designed to give you a capsulized understanding of what is happening in Earth and throughout our solar system at this critical time in galactic history. These discourses are purposely as brief and as simple as the subject matter will permit, so that you can quickly make this information available to others in as widespread and understandable a manner as possible. It is a matter of life and death that man of Earth begin to grasp quickly these changes that are taking place, and to understand how these changes will affect his own individual future for perhaps millions of years.

"To understand why Earth is in its present turmoil, we must flash back in time to the great civilization of Atlantis. Oh Yes ; Atlantis really existed ! Not as a figment of science fiction, but as a tangible civilization in Earth's past history.

"Man's purpose in experiencing life anywhere in the Universe is to grow in evolutionary experience and to master each phase in his eternal life. And how do we master the third dimensional environment of Earth? First, by getting to truly 'know oneselves'—who we are, what we are, why we are here. Second, by learning to control all aspects of this environment. Third, by understanding Earth and its relationship to what lies beyond the third dimensional environment.

"In Atlantis, man had advanced to a remarkable degree of control and understanding of this third dimensional environment, and was at a point where he could have led Earth and its inhabitants into the fourth dimensional experience of physical-spiritual growth. Instead, some who possessed advanced knowledge began to abuse and pervert this knowledge by enslaving other men, and by misusing their spiritual powers in various other ways. When this abuse of spiritual power became too widespread, it set into motion certain karmic forces which resulted in the eventual disintegration and destruction of the civilization. This destruction did not occur in one giant cataclysm, as may be commonly supposed. Rather, it occurred as a process of decline that lasted over thousands of years. During this period of degeneration, the continent gradually broke apart and yielded its majority portions to the ocean. Gradually, the inhabitants of this once great civilization migrated to various parts of Earth, taking with them the remembered skills and technologies that resulted in the archeological wonders that fascinate us today. Modern archeology is for the most part at a loss to explain such evidences as still exist in Central and South America, in England and Egypt and elsewhere around Earth. Eventually the memory of the glorious civilization that once existed, faded entirely except in the awareness of the adepts who possessed the arcanum, and in the subconscious minds of former Atlanteans.

"What has all of this to do with unfolding Divine Plan? Just this—Atlantis was not the only great civilization that has evolved upon Earth. There have been others lost to antiquity such as Lemuria. Each time that mankind has advanced to the level of a Lemuria or an Atlantis, it has had within its reach the opportunity to raise Earth's level of consciousness to fourth dimensional awareness and it has failed. Each failure was due to the misuse of spiritual powers.

"In the past, this could be condoned because there was still another chance. Now, however, we have reached a point in Earth's history and in galactic evolution where the transition into fourth dimensional consciousness must be made.

"Let me explain. The Divine Plan is based upon the Will of God (Spirit, Universal Mind, or whatever name you choose to call the indefinable Infinite Intelligence). Divine Mind always proceeds in an orderly, evolutionary pattern predicated upon Its principles of Universal Law. Wherever this Divine Plan affects man, he is always made aware so that he will have the opportunity to cooperate and grow upward in this evolutionary spiral.

"Man is now being made aware, through many means (such as this discourse) of certain galactic facts of universal, immortal life. As you know, our solar system is a part of the Milky Way galaxy. Our solar system revolves around the Milky Way in an orbit that takes 206 million years as you calculate time. Let us refer to this revolution of our solar system around the galaxy as the Great Cycle Orbit. Our solar system was created over 4½ billion years ago. This corresponds to 22 Great Cycle Orbits of our solar system around the Great Central Sun of the Milky Way. In the Will of Divine Mind, as communicated to the Spiritual Hierarchy of our solar system, this completes the time cycle in which our entire solar system is to remain in its present state of evolution. As the Aquarian Age dawns, we begin to move into a new orbit around the Great Central Sun, and to move into a new vibration where no expression below the fourth dimension can continue to exist.

"Man first began to experience life in our solar system 206 million years ago, at the beginning of the present Great Cycle Orbit. The Divine Plan is for all human life within our solar system to achieve at least the awareness of cosmic consciousness by the end of this orbit which is reaching its conclusion now with the end of the Piscean Age. This means that man of Earth must immediately become aware of what cosmic consciousness is and take the necessary steps to raise his individual level of consciousness to that state of awareness. Failure to do so will result in self destruction! Man of Earth, in his present state, simply cannot tolerate the new incoming vibration.

"Within this Great Cycle Orbit, there have been a number of lesser cycles. When the Atlantean civilization failed to reach its development potential, this left only the 26,000 year minor cycle of the zodiac to complete the Plan. As the present Piscean Age draws to a close, this 26,000 year cycle, concurrently with the Great Cycle Orbit, comes to an end.

"At this moment, planet Earth is the only planet in our solar system where man has not yet reached the cosmic level of awareness. This level of consciousness must now be rapidly attained in order to fulfill the Divine Plan.

"Now, at this point you may be a bit perplexed, Joseph. You may be thinking, 'I could go along with a lot of these ideas, but when he starts talking about human life on all the other planets of our solar system, that's too much. Our space probes haven't revealed any human life or civilization on any other planets.' And my answer to your thoughts, Joseph, is that you limit yourself to UN-REALITY when you rely solely upon your five physical senses, and upon the findings of conventional Earth science, to tell you whether or not intelligent human life exists on the other planets of our solar system. Not only is there human life on the other planets of our solar system, but the inhabitants are generally more evolved than you of Earth. Furthermore, they are in communication with each other, and in some instances with people on Earth. It is because this communication does exist, much the same as you are presently experiencing, that you can be aware of the reality of the above statements. THOSE WHO DOUBT AND DENY THESE POSSIBILITIES, ARE THOSE WHO HAD BEST START DEVELOPING THEIR OWN HIGHER SENSES!

"When Atlantis was at its height, there was open communication between Earth and the other planets of our solar system. After the fall, however, this open communication was removed. Now that man of Earth has again evolved to a point where he can make the transition into fourth dimensional consciousness, communication and contacts with extraterrestrial beings has greatly increased.

"Yes, my beloved Joseph, there is a Plan. This Plan involves many beings, human and otherwise, from within and without the Earth's planetary structure. It will behoove all men to open their minds and their hearts to at least *consider* these possibilities. It will be far better to cooperate and work with the Divine Plan and to reap the Divine Love, Light, Life, Peace, Truth and Joy that it offers, than to oppose it and reap eons of misery and regrets!"

"I am profoundly impressed by your discourse, Kut Humi, and with the ideas which you have expressed. It is difficult for me to believe that anyone hearing what you have just told me could ignore it or cast it aside without further investigation. It would take an extremely prejudiced and unthinking mind to simply disregard this information."

"There are many wise and beautiful souls upon our Earth. When they are made aware of an intelligent Divine Plan, they will want to participate in bringing the Plan into fruition. The most difficult obstacle for most of them will probably be to scale those orthodox walls of entrapment. The second most difficult obstacle will probably be to rise above the self-imposed limitation of relying only upon the five physical senses.

"In future discourses, Joseph, you will see how the Divine Plan is already working to remove these barriers. In the meantime, be unrelenting in your own efforts to attain custody of the Treasure of El Dorado!"

"Thank you, Kut Humi."

"Peace be with you, Joseph."

CHAPTER 6

The Unfolding Plan—Part III

Hilarion Speaks on
UFO's

Why They Are Here

Following Kut Humi's discourses concerning Atlantis and life on the other planets of our solar system, I immersed myself totally in my studies and meditation.

In my studies, I was increasingly drawn to a closer examination of literature dealing with esoteric matters. In the course of my readings, I began to find that I now possessed an intuitive faculty that permitted me to grasp abstruse concepts which had hitherto been hidden from by understanding. Delighted with this realization, I voraciously absorbed some of Earth's greatest literature dealing with profound hidden truths.

The more I read and meditated, the more I realized that most of Earth's greatest literature had been channeled through its writers, either with or without the conscious awareness of the writer. There is an unmistakable thread and pattern that weaves throughout the esoteric writings, that reveals itself to an awakened mind as the template of the Divine Plan.

Upon reaching such a realization, I then began to see the Divine Imprint upon everything. I began to grasp the causes that lay behind external appearances. I began to understand cause and effect.

Absorbed as I was in my efforts, it suddenly came as a shock for me to realize that El Dorado had not manifested himself in a mental communication to me in three months. It was then that I fully understood that he had never left my side during this time. It was his presence, his inspiration, his motivation that was giving me the energy, direction and the comprehension in everything that I was doing.

Still, it was a great thrill when El Dorado announced to me:

"Joseph, it is an opportune moment for a discourse on another aspect of the Divine Plan."

"I can't tell you how pleased and happy I am to hear you again, El Dorado. I have been constantly aware of your presence for the past three months as you guided me in my development, but nevertheless I love it when you manifest yourself to me in this manner. What is going to be the subject of today's discourse?"

"With me today, Joseph, is the Master Teacher, Hilarion, who comes to speak to you about extraterrestrial spacecraft. As you know, it is a topic of great controversy. Many, perhaps most people, do not really believe that the so-called UFO's are extraterrestrial. Many who do believe they are, are often labeled as borderline schizophrenic or otherwise maligned or defamed. And even among the believers themselves, there are few who truly understand the nature and mission of the extraterrestrial presence on Earth.

"The purpose of today's discourse is to give you additional insights into their presence that you are to share with mankind.

"Before Hilarion begins, it is appropriate for you to know that he too was mentioned in Sananda's discourse. He was incarnated as Plato and as Paul the Apostle. One of Hilarion's major responsibilities within the Spiritual Hierarchy is to unify many diverse facets in implementing the Divine Plan. This entails integrating and coordinating various planetary forces on the physical and astral levels to bring about a smooth transition into the 23rd Great Cycle Orbit. The main focus at this time in this unification and integration process is to awaken man of Earth to the reality of human life throughout our solar system.

"I am indeed honored to present my fellow Christ and very dear friend, Hilarion."

As was my experience with El Dorado, Sananda and Kut Humi, I was overwhelmed by an ecstatic, and rapturous feeling as Hilarion entered by aura. The thought crossed my mind that one could easily become spoiled by Masters coming regularly into their auric force fields. The closest comparable sensation is sexual intercourse. However, that description is rather inadequate as unfortunately, sexual intercourse usually lacks the involvement of one's total being that occurs when one's aura is overshadowed by a Christed being or an Angelic being.

Hilarion, reading my thoughts, said to me:

"The goal of mankind on Earth, Joseph, is to reach full cosmic consciousness. As one attains this state of being, one is continuously enveloped in the vibration that you are now experiencing. In this state of being, one is in 'heaven' wherever one happens to be."

"Attaining cosmic consciousness is certainly my goal, Hilarion, but I do not know what steps to take to attain it."

"Continue as you are doing in your commitment and dedication to serving the Divine Plan, and you will be shown the way. For the moment, your development requires that you understand the Unfolding Plan more fully. To this end, I will speak to you of the purpose of the extraterrestrial presence on Earth.

"Do you recall Kut Humi's statement; 'When Atlantis was at its height, there was open communication between Earth and the other planets of our solar system,' and 'Now that man of Earth has again evolved to a point where he can make the transition into the fourth dimensional consciousness, communication and contacts with extraterrestrials has greatly increased'?"

"Yes, I remember that statement."

"Good. No serious researcher into the existence of extraterrestrial spacecraft can long doubt their reality. The worldwide evidence is simply too massive and too well documented to ignore. Therefore, the main thrust of the serious researcher's effort must soon shift from whether they exist to why they are here. The press and popular books on the subject resort to all kinds of incorrect speculation in this matter. Their conjectures range from the macabre to the absurd.

"The real reason for the presence of extraterrestrials is nowhere to be found in the press or news media, in spite of repeated messages to channels around Earth. Simply stated, their purpose in being here is to help reawaken man of Earth to the reality and actuality of Universal Life, and to help unfold the Divine Plan as it relates to life in our solar system.

"The presence of extraterrestrials should be one of the most reassuring events that is taking place on Earth. Instead, it is often the cause of great fear and apprehension. Fear is born of ignorance. Were it not so, people would welcome their space brothers with open arms. No doubt, they will be more welcome when their presence is better understood.

87

"Many changes are required to prepare Earth for the Aquarian Age. The space brothers are prepared to assist in many ways, once their presence is understood and accepted.

"As stated previously by Kut Humi, our whole solar system is moving into a new Great Cycle Orbit within its galaxy of the Milky Way. In this new cycle, our entire solar system will be functioning at a higher dimensional vibration and expression. As the galactic timetable rapidly unfolds when this orderly evolution is to take place, all planets of the solar system are prepared except Earth. Since Earth is the laggard, it is quite natural that the inhabitants of our sister planets should direct their attention and efforts to Earth and render whatever aid is necessary short of outright interference. Until now, such aid has consisted primarily in the following: 1. Communicating through channels like you with the hope that their messages would receive wide publication, and 2. making frequent appearances around Earth so that their spacecraft would be visible to large numbers of people.

"Quite obviously, these efforts have not been altogether successful. Fear and consternation have greeted most spacecraft appearances. For years their presence has met with official governmental silence. When anyone in government did speak out, it was to deny their extraterrestrial character and to explain away the incidents as some type of natural phenomena. (The irony here, of course, is that they are a natural phenomena; though not perceived as such by the inhibited Earth intellect). All major governments of Earth have repeatedly received information through various channels to explain the extraterrestrial presence. These have been ignored as the product of a deranged mind. Surely, at some point, someone must come to the realization that the 'problem' of the existence of spacecraft is not going to disappear because man of Earth officially refuses to recognize their presence.

"Public acceptance is not promoted when 'contactees' react to the presence of spacecraft with terror. The account of a terrified contactee can rarely be expected to reflect actual circumstances. Their very terror precludes rational explanation of the encounter. But the whole point is that if the general populace were educated to the realities of life in our solar system, people might not react with such fear to the presence of extraterrestrial beings.

"Let us proceed further into a clearer understanding.

"As Kut Humi has told you, every planet in our solar system is inhabited by human beings. Don't be misled by the fact that this human life has not yet been detected by the three dimensional scientific instruments of Earth. Just as Kirlian photography reveals 'auras' that the untrained human eye is unable to discern, instruments will soon be invented which can 'see' this life that exists in the other planetary vibrations. Until that time, any rational person should at least give serious thought to the possibility of human life existing in an environment beyond the observation of one not attuned to that particular physical vibration.

"So, the fact is that every planet in our solar system is inhabited by human beings. They have physical bodies just as Earth man has a physical body, but their different vibration renders them invisible to your three dimensional, sensual eyes. Their civilizations, their knowledge, their life styles, vary from planet to planet, but they are all in a state of spiritual evolution more advanced than man of Earth.

"Isn't it only natural and desirable that life should vary from planet to planet? After all, we are all immortal creatures. Wouldn't it be hell if all that we could look forward to upon the physical planets was lifetime after lifetime of the same boring experience? In fact, let's just look at the situation on Earth. Don't knowledge, culture, life style, customs, opportunities, etc., differ considerably from one country to another, from region to region, even from one neighborhood to another? Don't we all get tired of routine at times and try to 'get away from it all' by taking a vacation in a different setting?

"In the more advanced life styles that exist on other planets, people no longer select their leaders in a political manner. Their level of consciousness has progressed beyond that method of government. In their more advanced state of consciousness they can readily discern who among them is most qualified to lead. Leadership then naturally falls to those individuals. One could best describe this leadership as spiritual rather than political. However, it is not spiritual in any religious sense. It is spiritual in the sense of fuller use of inherent spiritual faculties as distinguished from the sensory intellectual approach of Earth. It is a much more orderly, fair, economical, ethical, effective and enlightened approach to government than that which Earth now practices.

"A still higher system of spiritual government exists within our solar system. This level of government is referred to as the Spiritual Hierarchy of the solar system. The Spiritual Hierarchy consists of the most spiritually advanced souls in the solar system, and it is composed of both human beings and angelic beings of very high development. It is the Spiritual Hierarchy that is in charge, so to speak, of the orderly evolution of all aspects of the Divine Plan within our solar system. It is they, more than anyone else, who can sense the transitional requirements necessary to keep our solar system in harmony with our galaxy. If you can accept this information, then it should not be difficult to accept that the Spiritual Hierarchy is very much concerned with bringing Earth quickly to a higher level of understanding.

"It is not my intention to go into any great detail in revealing the unfolding Plan. My objective is to give enough information so that you can at least discern the possibility of an overall, intelligently guided Divine Plan that affects the destinies of us all.

"The presence of spacecraft upon Earth is not a random, happenstance occurrence. It is an integral part of an overall program designed to bring Earth quickly into a state of higher understanding. The craft which you see in your skies come for the most part from your sister planets in the solar system. They operate primarily under the inspiration of the Spiritual Hierarchy.

"Occasionally, of course, Earth is visited by extra-terrestrials from beyond our solar system. They are usually not participants in this unfolding Plan. Furthermore, they are karmically bound to refrain from any interference with the evolution of Earth or with human life on the planet. When or if they do interfere, it is a personal act for which they are both responsible and accountable, the same as you would be accountable for violating the rights of anyone, anywhere, by the Universal law of karma.

"Now, let us try to understand more clearly why spacecraft of our own solar system are visiting Earth. Just as your own highly developed country, the United States of America, can look at its more backward neighbors in other parts of Earth and discern from experience, what they need to advance their understanding so, too, can your brothers from the more advanced planets view the conditions and needs of Earth. Imagine, for instance, trying to explain or demonstrate the technology of a camera, or a portable color videotape television, or a jet airliner, or a philosophical truth, to a primitive inhabitant of New Guinea, and you will have some idea of the difficulty facing the Spiritual Hierarchy and our space brothers in awakening man of Earth. When you approach primitive Earth people with the products of your more advanced minds and technologies, they will usually react with fear and panic. You can easily see that their reaction is based upon ignorance. Why is it then that you of Earth do not recognize that your own reaction to spacecraft is precisely the same?

"The spacecraft are here to help Earth! They are not here to harm Earth in any way. They are not here to conquer Earth because of a failure of the life support systems on their planets. They are not interested in having anyone for lunch! They do not need anything that Earth has except friendship, love and cooperation. They do not need to capture anyone for dissection or experimentation.

"Just think of the ideas and assistance that could be at your disposal if Earth would just stop rejecting its space brothers out of fear and ignorance!

"The space brothers are here to help man of Earth evolve to a higher state of consciousness and awareness. They are here to show man of Earth that human life is not limited to the planet Earth. They are here as 'signs in the skies' fulfilling scriptural prophecy heralding the 'latter days.' They are here to help Earth understand the great changes that will accompany the change in vibration that occurs as the solar system moves further into the new Great Cycle Orbit. They are here as part of a

91

vast plan affecting the entire solar system and its advancement in the galaxy. Consequently, what affects our solar system also affects the galaxy. They are here because they love their fellow man and want to help lift him up.

"Now, Joseph, I have a question for you. What will you think of the next time you see a so-called UFO?"

"I will be thinking primarily of the role UFO's are fulfilling in the enactment of the Divine Plan and I will be hoping that man will quickly begin to understand and accept their presence."

"That is good! May the divine light of truth encompass and protect you until we meet again, Joseph."

"Thank you for your enlightening instructions, Hilarion."

CHAPTER 7

The Unfolding Plan—Part IV

El Dorado Speaks On
The Bodies of Man

"My beloved Joseph, I come to you now in fulfillment of my obligation to guide you faithfully in the path of enlightenment.

"It is with sympathy, love and understanding that I watch you struggling to comprehend the wonder and complexity of yourself as a being of many parts. I have sat with you in your studies, your readings, your meditations, and your conversations with others. I have observed your confusion. Do not be discouraged. There are very few upon Earth at this time who have a clear comprehension of who and what they are as a person, as a human being, as a Son of God. Few indeed are aware of the totality of their being.

"You must understand that it is necessary for me to let you struggle to learn who and what you are. Only your sincere efforts can establish a basis for comprehension. You have reached a point beyond which you cannot proceed on your own. However, you are at a point where my revelations can be grasped. That is what is meant by the ancient and wise saying, 'When the student is ready, the teacher will appear'.

"I come to you now to deliver a most important discourse. Record this information carefully. Study it well. When you have mastered this knowledge, you will have reached a point of true cosmic conscious awareness. Beyond this point, your progress will depend upon your continued dedication to truth and higher principles.

"Let me now explain to you the parts and the potentials of all human beings developing within this solar system. For the sake of simplicity, I will use the term 'body' when referring to any of the parts of the total self.

"The various bodies which constitute the total potential of all human beings developing within this solar system are the physical matter body, the astral antimatter body, the christ body, the antichrist body, the angelic body, the archangelic body, the mental body and the emotional body.

"The astral antimatter body balances and complements the physical matter body. Likewise, the antichrist and archangelic bodies balance and complement their counterpart bodies.

"The mental and emotional bodies are integral components of all of the bodies of the total self. Those who can accept and work with this knowledge will make rapid progress in their spiritual growth and understanding. Those who cannot must unfortunately suffer the effects of their obduracy.

"As we have been telling you, certain things are going to take place whether man is ready or not. We are going to see to it that we keep our part of the bargain by providing mankind with sufficient information. What man subsequently does with the information will determine both his own personal future as well as the future of planet Earth.

"Moving onward, let us explore briefly the various aspects or bodies that comprise the total person in his solar system development.

"First, let us look at the physical body. It is clearly the most magnificent and complicated instrument in Earth today. It is a marvel of mechanical, chemical and electrical symmetry and artistry. It has been brilliantly interwoven by the Creator to form a suitable vehicle through which man can manifest himself within the physical vibrations of Earth.

"Your physical body is merely the operable vehicle or instrument through which your other bodies express their functions while you are incarnated upon Earth. The physical body is not 'you' in any complete sense. It is most important for people to begin to grasp this fundamental truth. Just as you would get in an automobile to go from one place to another, when you are incarnated on the physical planets you enter into a physical body to make your sojourn of a lifetime. Just as you have to learn to drive an automobile before one can complete a successful journey, so you must learn to operate the physical body properly in order to enjoy a successful lifetime.

"You do not think of yourself as an automobile merely because you are using one as a means of conveyance. Likewise, it is quite ignorant to think of yourself only in terms of a physical body or personality merely because the real you is manifested through such a body.

"Just as the automobile will be shaped by the care and attention that you give it, so too will your physical body respond to your care or neglect. It is therefore vitally important to remember that with proper treatment, your physical body will serve you troublefree for a lifetime. With enlightened treatment, the physical body can be transmuted for all eternity, and not have to suffer a physical death. This is the truth.

"Existing within and around the physical body are imperishable bodies of which very few people are aware. These other bodies interpenetrate the physical body as well as extend beyond it. They have a tremendous effect on the health and well-being of the physical body. Whenever any of these other bodies are out of balance, this will be reflected as an illness in the physical body and personality.

"It is these other bodies that constitute the phenomenon referred to as an aura. When physical death occurs, these other bodies leave the physical body as a unit and become the operable vehicle through which the consciousness continues to function in other dimensions. It is also possible for these bodies to leave the physical body without the occurrence of death. This is accomplished through astral projection.

"It is imperative to keep in mind that true mastery of the physical dimensions can happen only when one has resurrected the physical body. This resurrection must take place through the conscious transformation of the physical body by changing its atomic structure. In accomplishing this, one's vibration is changed from third to fourth dimension. You will learn more about this in a later discourse.

"Whereas the physical body is the sacred temple containing the other bodies while one is physically incarnated, the astral body houses the other bodies after the transition called death. Unlike the physical body, however, the astral body is inviolable.

"You will find a number of terms used to describe the astral body, such as the soul body, the subconscious, the akashic, the causal and others. We prefer the term astral, since we consider the other terms too limiting and as being aspects or functions of the astral.

"The astral body, as we have said, is the operable vehicle through which one is manifested in the astral realms or dimensions. You will recall from your own astral travels while asleep, that the astral body is no less real than the physical body is thought to be.

"Now let us examine some of the functions which the various aspects of the astral body serve while one is physically incarnated. First, let us look at the subconscious. The subconscious is the mechanism which performs those vital functions that produce automatic actions and reactions on the physical level. Examples of this would be breathing, beating of the heart, blinking of the eyelids, eating, digesting, etc. All learned responses are also triggered from the subconscious. It is the subconscious which permits the formation of habits. It is the subconscious which must be re-programmed in order to break habits.

"The subconscious, in addition to being a part of the astral body, is also a component of the mind or mental body. This can cause great confusion in understanding the functions of the various bodies. That is why I have told you to study this discourse well. As a component of the mental body, the subconscious has the ability and the capacity to record all sensual, mental, emotional and spiritual experiences and to 'play back' this information upon request. In this respect, it functions like a tape recorder. Although the subconscious is a level of the mental body, it does not have the capacity for rational thought that the conscious or superconscious levels of mind have.

"The subconscious is to the astral body and the mental body what the brain is to the physical body, except of course that the subconscious is permanent. The physical brain is the storehouse or computer memory bank of the mortal self while physically incarnated. During one's physical incarnation, everything that one experiences is recorded in the brain. Likewise, everything that is recorded in the brain is also recorded in the subconscious.

"The subconscious does not have the capacity to discern what is true or false, good or bad or to differentiate between other extremes. It functions as a storehouse of information and a trigger for learned responses. Hence the importance of learning to properly program the subconscious with truth and to purge it of all erroneous knowledge and bad habits. Hence the pain and difficulty of *unlearning!* Hence the absolute necessity of understanding that the subconscious contains total memory information from all previous lives and experiences.

"With this understanding, one can recognize the effect of previous life experiences on one's present life and one's total well-being. When you begin to realize the massive amount of misinformation that can be, and usually is, stored in the subconscious, then you become aware of the urgent need to begin the unlearning process.

"At this point, I must make you aware of a subtle truth concerning the relationship of the conscious to the subconscious. I have told you that the subconscious is not capable of rational thinking and that it is a storehouse of information and a trigger for learned responses. If an individual's conscious mind does not exercise its prerogative for thinking, planning and executing instructions, then the subconscious will take over this function through its own triggering mechanism. In other words, the subconscious will in effect rule the conscious because the conscious fails to fulfill its responsibility to rule.

"You can see countless examples of this happening in the daily lives of those around you. Take, for instance, an individual raised in an atmosphere of bigotry where he was taught to hate all members of another race or religion. The individual has developed a very entrenched learned response that causes him to speak out in hatred, and contempt of those groups whom he has been taught to hate. This is the subconscious dominating the conscious. If the conscious were dominant, then the bigoted individual would think through the distorted reasons for his hate response and would realize the error of his subconscious prejudices.

"The subconscious has another singularly elusive but vitally significant function that you must comprehend —that is its ability to act as a conduit between the conscious and the superconscious. The superconscious is always seeking to contact the conscious. In order to reach the conscious, the superconscious must travel through the subconscious.

"We might compare the conscious to a light bulb, the subconscious to the electric wire and the superconscious to the energy source. The energy has to reach the light bulb before the light will shine. If the electric wire is shorted out or otherwise damaged, then the energy will not reach the light bulb and lighting or enlightenment will not occur. Going back to the subconscious, if it is impaired by an overload of misinformation, distorted learned responses and if it is in control of the conscious by default, then it is unlikely that superconscious energy will be able to reach the conscious effectively.

"What is being said here is that no one is going to make any real headway in his development until he begins to clear out the debris from his subconscious memory banks!

"One final analogy should serve to dramatize the necessity of cleansing the subconscious. Let the trap of a sink represent the subconscious. Let the area above the sink represent the superconscious and the pipe below the trap represent the conscious. What happens when the trap becomes clogged with sludge and debris? There is no light coming through — no clear water. Note what happens when the trap is unstopped. The sludge and debris is washed 'down' the pipes. In other words the blockage must be removed from below. The pressure is coming from above, representing the superconscious, but the removal takes place when the blockage passes through the pipe below the trap. In this analogy, it is the conscious which must recognize and eliminate the blockage by cooperating with the force from above.

"Let us now consider for a moment that quality of the astral body that is called soul. Think, if you will, of a cassette tape. When the tape is blank, it can be said to contain no soul. Now let us place the tape in a recorder and fill it with recordings. What we have done is to impart attributes to a previously empty cassette. We have given it soul.

"When one enters a new realm in a new body such as a newborn infant incarnating in Earth, the tape is blank. As one progresses through a lifetime, the tape becomes filled with all of the traits of personality, experience, learning, pleasure, pain, etc., that normally accompanies a lifetime. When the life ends, the tape is filled with that essence called soul.

"Within the total soul are many completed tapes containing the records of all incarnational experiences. As you are now beginning to appreciate, the completed tapes form the memory bank, or the akashic record of an individual being. Keep in mind that all of these completed tapes are in an active file and are hooked up to your inner computer. Therefore, whatever information is contained on any tapes, whether it be good or evil, true or false, right or wrong, correct or incorrect, can and does influence your well-being in your present life.

"This is why many people go through lifetime after lifetime making the same mistakes over and over again. The cumulative impressions etched upon their souls produces subtle impulses that trigger activities which a weak, unaware and undeveloped conscious mind fails to control.

"The only possible way to correct this condition is to become aware of its existence and then to take necessary steps to unlearn, re-program and replace all of the defective recordings. This is a painful process because it always involves the replacing of cherished erroneous concepts with truth and higher understanding.

"Even upon reaching this level of awareness, most people are just too lazy or procrastinating to follow through with corrective measures. Perhaps it will aid them in their resolve and self-discipline to know that even laziness and procrastination are themselves erroneous patterns which must be overcome and purged from the soul by positive action.

"In summary, the subconscious and the soul lack discernment. They cannot reason. They cannot think. By their nature, however, they can control the conscious by feeding back any information that is stored within. If the conscious mind does not exercise its obligation to control input into the subconscious and into the soul, the latter will always control the conscious to a greater or lesser degree.

"Of the spiritual, or non-physical bodies, the astral body has the lowest vibration. It is the astral body that is normally seen by clairvoyants with their spiritual or third eye. It is also the astral body that some psychics are given the capacity to 'read'. By means of such readings, many people have become aware of reincarnation through the revelation of one or most past lives.

"With sufficient training, awareness and understanding, everyone can go into his akashic record and discover many things about himself. As the vibrations of Earth continue to rise, this ability becomes ever more practical.

"As I have indicated earlier, there are three distinct, yet inseparable levels of the mental body or mind. Once you have understood the significance of the subconscious and the soul, Joseph, you are ready to take conscious control of your destiny. To take conscious control effectively, you must utilize the conscious aspect of the mental body as fully as possible.

"The conscious part of your mental body provides you with great powers of thinking. Thinking is the capacity to discern, reason, rationalize, to exercise self-discipline, to deduce, to employ logic, to analyze, inquire, synthesize, judge, investigate, cognize, observe, etc. In short, thinking can provide consciousness of your self and of your environment with the potential for limitless development in the cosmos and eternity.

"In exercising the abilities of the conscious mind, it must rely upon the physical brain while incarnated. The brain can be precisely compared to a computer. It is, in fact, the most sophisticated computer in Earth. The brain itself, of course, is not the mind. It is one of the instruments that the mind uses while you are manifested in the physical planes of expression. Hence you can see at this point, the dire necessity of maintaining the total physical body in the most perfect condition possible. Any imbalance in the physical body affecting the brain, the nervous system or the spiritual centers, will keep the conscious mind from performing its functions properly.

"The brain is the memory bank for the experiences you have while physically incarnated. And, as I have already stated, the subconscious mind is the memory bank for your total experiences. Whatever is recorded in the brain, is recorded automatically in the subconscious as well. That which is in the subconscious, however, is not *necessarily* in the brain. We bring data from the subconscious into the brain through the meditative process and through opening various other doorways to memory. Once the conscious mind is made aware of this process, then it can make tremendous strides in controlling the development of the mortal self.

"You see, Joseph, you are constantly having experiences in the astral body and in the etheric (or Christ) body which are not recorded in the brain, because these experiences take place while the consciousness is outside of the physical body. Because these experiences are not recorded in the brain, you do not recall them on the mortal conscious level. These experiences can be recorded in the brain, however, if you are able to reach into the subconscious and become aware of them. And that, after all, is the primary function of the mind or mental body—to produce awareness! This ability, then, becomes an incredible tool in the development of your potential.

"The mental body has three distinct parts or levels as I have indicated earlier, the conscious, the subconscious and the superconscious. These are the qualities of mind that govern individualized man. Beyond this is Universal Mind, which will be explained in a subsequent discourse.

"Mastery of the physical dimensions requires not only awareness of the existence of your superconscious mind power, but it also requires the ability to communicate with this level of mind. Within the framework of the Divine Plan for man of Earth, however, you are not required to master the physical dimension completely, though many will want to do this. What is required is that man of Earth become aware of the existence of the power of the superconscious mind and desire its attainment.

"Man cannot possibly reach this level or even desire its attainment until he first knows of it, and then realizes that he has the potential to master it.

"Viewing man's present state of awareness in Earth, this will give you some idea of the magnitude of the task that confronts those of us who are pledged to help enlighten mankind.

"To give you some idea of the scope of the superconscious mind, Joseph, think of a rating scale numbered from 1 to 10 as representing the range of man's conscious mind in Earth. Then classify the most outstanding geniuses of Earth history using 10 as the ultimate that is attainable. You will find that such men as Einstein,

Swedenborg, Balzac, Whitman, etc., would be rated from perhaps 7 through 9. By comparison, a pure state of superconsciousness would range into the hundreds or thousands. In this comparison you must keep in mind that the purest state of superconsciousness is that state in which the superconscious mind is joined with Universal Mind. Christ Jesus of Nazareth would be the best example of one who demonstrated the superconscious mind. It is quite easy to conclude from this, is it not, that the means exist to literally transform Earth into a paradise by educating mankind as to its potential?

"Next we will look at the emotional body. Just what is its purpose and function?

"It is the emotional body that gives you a feeling nature. It is the feeling nature that produces the capacity for experiencing all levels of emotion such as joy and sorrow, love and hate, compassion and malevolence, ecstasy and depression, pleasure and pain, excitement and indifference. The degree to which these and other traits attain the heights and depths will determine the vividness of the experience being felt, and the strength of the impression recorded upon the soul memory.

"As we experience life, this is how we truly learn right from wrong, good from bad. It takes only one good burn, for example, to teach us not to place our hand in the fire. Once we have burned ourself, the pain of that memory and experience is sufficient to deter us from repeating it. Gradually, as we begin to mature, we intuitively seek a way of living and expressing ourselves that will lead us permanently away from the emotional depths of pain, and lead us instead into the heights of joy. This is clearly the pathway that leads to higher consciousness.

"The emotional or feeling capacity is experienced on all levels of expression. On the physical level, it can be experienced as a purely physical manifestation such as heat or cold, pain from a physical injury, touching, etc. It can be experienced mentally by perceiving joy, happiness, excitement, hate, etc. It can be experienced physically and mentally, at the same time, by enjoying a party with good friends where delicious foods are eaten, by engaging in sexual union with a loved one, by fighting an enemy, etc.

104

"No one would want to live without the emotional body. It would be pointless to exist without the capacity to feel. No attainment could bring any satisfaction since satisfaction itself is an emotional quality. When viewed individually, it becomes increasingly obvious that each aspect of our total Self is indispensable to the function and purpose of our total being.

"Next, we will look at the christ body. The christ body has been variously described by enlightened writers through the ages as the light body, the ascended body, the oversoul, the high self, the I Am, the resurrected body, the electric body, the superconscious body, the Son (Sun) of God, the etheric body and various other terms.

"The terms light body and electric body come closest to describing this body in scientific language. The I Am body and the christ body perhaps come closest to describing it in spiritual terms.

"From the scientific viewpoint, the terms light body or the electric body would best describe the effect produced in the atomic structure of this body by the speed of the electron movement within the atoms. This speed equals or exceeds the speed of light. The body itself, wherever it is manifested, gives off a brilliant white light.

"In keeping with the Divine Plan to educate and enlighten man of Earth, there have been many instances of christed beings appearing to mankind all around Earth. One superb recent example of this phenomenon, for instance, took place in Zeitoun, a suburb of Cairo, Egypt, between 1968 and 1971. It was there, at St. Mary's Church, that Mary (Jesus' mother) appeared frequently and was seen and photographed by thousands of persons over a three year period. These appearances usually took place at night. The light from Mary's body was so brilliant that it illuminated the whole area surrounding the church.

"While most people who witnessed this happening look upon it as a miracle, the time has come for people to stop limiting their understanding and begin to look beyond their present three-dimensional myopia. There is really no such thing as a miracle. What people call a miracle or supernatural occurrence is in reality a normal, natural event caused by the application of immutable universal laws by beings of greater understanding and awareness than those who are witnessing the 'miracle'.

"From the spiritual viewpoint, the I Am and the christ body are terms that seem to best explain this body. The simplest way to describe the I Am is to say that it is a statement of one's absolute realization of who and what one is in cosmic terms. The term christ means 'the anointed one'. When one attains the level of Christhood, this singularly important event is accompanied by a recognition ceremony initiated in the Angelic and Christ realms, wherein the new Christ is properly recognized and advanced to the status of Christhood.

"Achieving the status of Christhood confers upon the recipient many powers not found in the lesser bodies or aspects of our being. Again, Jesus presents the best example in contemporary Earth history of the Christ powers and talents. Among the powers Jesus was known to have demonstrated were the following: bilocation (being in two or more places simultaneously), levitation (overcoming gravity), manifestation and precipitation (the use of pure energy to bring something into physical manifestation; an example of this was the multiplication of bread and fish), control of elemental forces (quieting the storm and putting out the fire), materialization and dematerialization (the ability to change vibration from one dimension to another causing one to disappear), teleportation (converting matter into energy and transporting it through space to another location). In addition to the above examples, Jesus also demonstrated many other spiritual (psychic) abilities such as healing, prophesy, telekinesis, apport, psychometry, mental communication, astral projection, etc. In teaching and demonstrating these Christ talents, Jesus constantly reminded his followers that they could do all of these and even greater things.

"Were this not so, Jesus would not have stated it. He is Earth's greatest teacher and he has never been known to lie. So the simple truth is that everyone has the potential of becoming a Christ. You will not, however, achieve Christhood through the efforts of another. You will achieve it by your own efforts or not at all. The doctrine of vicarious redemption (the false concept that Jesus died for everyone's sins, and therefore all you have to do is to accept Jesus as your Lord and Saviour to be saved) may be comforting to its advocates, but it will never advance one a single step towards self-mastery! Vicarious redemption is contrary to the universal law of cause and effect.

"It is vitally important for the progress of Earth, Joseph, that people begin to understand that they possess a Christ Self. This Christ Self is constantly trying to guide and influence the mortal consciousness to follow the path that leads to superconsciousness. One's Christ Self might be compared to a puppeteer. One's mortal physical self might be compared to the puppet. The puppeteer creates, guides and cares for the puppet. The puppet on the other hand is not even aware of the existence of the puppeteer. As man goes through life in Earth's physical and astral realms, he is most often unaware of who and what he is. You might compare him to the puppet in the puppet show. In actuality, the puppet doesn't know what is coming next. It is participating in a play but is not aware of the plot. Likewise, man of Earth is participating in a great cosmic drama and for the most part is totally unaware of the plot or the players or the consequences of an unsuccessful show! The Christ Self is always trying to communicate to its mortal self, but usually the communication lines are tangled up by a distorted subconscious. It could be compared to the puppet show when the strings become entangled and the puppet is no longer able to respond to the guidance of the puppeteer.

"So you see, Joseph, we have a most difficult task in reaching the conscious mind of man of Earth. Man's stubborn resistance to the truth throughout the centuries is proof of the difficulty involved in reprogramming the subconscious mind. Man does not change his habits easily.

"The superconscious is the functioning mind of the Christ Self. In the Christ levels of expression, the Christ Self, through its mind power, is able to commune much more effectively with Universal Mind than are the purely physical or astral levels. Accordingly, one has much greater knowledge and understanding as a Christ and is in a much better position to guide, direct and assist man of Earth.

"We want you to know unequivocally that it is possible to achieve Christhood while still incarnated in the physical or astral vibrations.

"Whoever does achieve Christhood, will no longer be subject to the laws that govern those levels, but will be subject to the transcendent laws of the Christ vibrations.

"Furthermore, we want you to know that when one achieves the full Christ vibration, then physical death will no longer have dominion over him. He will have literally conquered the physical vibrations and can freely travel through the physical, astral and Christ vibrations. This mastery gives him the power to alter his vibration at will from physical through astral to Christ vibration.

"In this discourse, we will not dwell on any description of the antichrist body. The antichrist body will be discussed in a future discourse.

"An understanding of the angelic and archangelic bodies is not necessary at man's present state of evolution and therefore is not to appear as part of this discourse in any book that you may write. Suffice it to say what these bodies constitute man's potential as he continues to evolve within this solar system.

"When you reach a full understanding of the knowledge contained in this discourse, Joseph, I think that you will possess sufficient cosmic conscious awareness to progress easily to the next step in your development."

"Thank you, El Dorado. Many questions have been answered by this discourse. Many things that have puzzled me all of my life have now been made clear. I will study this information until I understand it thoroughly."

CHAPTER 8

The Unfolding Plan—Part V

Djwhal Khul Speaks on
Health

With the aid of the discourses, it was becoming progressively easier to grasp the fact that there was an overall Divine Plan to raise the conscious awareness of mankind upon Earth. It had become obvious to me that if there were a Divine Plan, it would require the cooperation of man of Earth to fulfill it. In order to fulfill it, it will require some knowledge of it.

I then began to examine my own progress. As I reflected upon the changes in my awareness, I was stunned both by the scope and the magnitude of the changes that had taken place in a relatively few years. There were major changes in my health, in my practice of religion, in my philosophies, in my attitudes about everything. Accompanying these changes, and perhaps precipitating them, were tremendous changes in my so-called psychic abilities and capacities.

At this point, I began to reflect deeply upon the influence of my psychic capacities on my overall growth and change in awareness. I thought back five years ago. At that time, I was in rather poor condition physically, mentally and emotionally. Reinforcing my poor condition was an appalling list of bad habits that had gained control of me over the years. Most of you know the feeling I am sure. You just continually put off breaking a bad habit that you know is undermining your health. You keep saying to yourself "Next month or next year (or some vague time in the future) I am going to quit doing that." Only next month or next year never arrives. Meantime we keep piling on more bad habits, until the sheer weight of our self-abuse takes its toll. Let me list a few of my own bad habits.

I drank 8 to 10 cups of coffee daily. I smoked 1 to 2 packs of cigarettes daily. I stuffed myself with candy of which I kept an ample supply in my dresser drawer at all times. No meal was complete without plenty of meat. Fresh fruits and vegetables were seldom on my menu. By constantly putting it off, I had given up regular exercise. Ice Cream and snack foods also contributed to my overweight and undernourished condition.

Added to these bad physical habits, I had my share of negative mental and emotional attitudes and hangups.

At this time, I was a regular churchgoer and was seriously 'practicing' my religion. In retrospect, it seems quite strange that I found little inconsistency between my awful habits and my religion. Perhaps this was because I had so much company.

In any event, I did reach a point in dissipation where my body and spirit rebelled. The combination of all of my physical, mental and emotional self-abuse joined to produce a state of such misery, that it brought me to the verge of a complete breakdown.

It was at this point near despair that I reached out for help. I went to my doctor. I suppose that I was seeking some magic potion that would cure all of my problems overnight.

After a cursory examination, my doctor stated that nothing was physically wrong with me. At this point, I felt so horrible that I simply could not believe that there could be nothing wrong with me physically. As the doctor looked blandly at me, I broke down and started to cry. I was that close to physical exhaustion and nervous collapse. As I sought to regain my composure, the doctor soothingly suggested that I allow him to make an appointment with a psychiatrist. He assured me that there was no stigma attached to psychiatric treatment and urged me to avail myself of this aid. In spite of my distress, I was certain that I did not require psychiatric care. I told my doctor that I would think about it for a few days, then I went home.

That night, I sat up late after everyone else had gone to bed. I could not begin to describe my misery. I suffered constantly from heartburn, indigestion, constipation, insomnia, irritability, impatience, outburst of temper, severe allergenic reactions, headaches, depression, jealousy, hate, resentment, a total lack of energy and assorted other symptoms. As I sat alone that night I contemplated the incredible variety of ailments that beset me and wondered how in the world a doctor could fail to find something wrong with me physically. I thought to myself, "life is definitely not worth continuing if I must suffer like this any longer." Then I said aloud softly, "Please help me, someone. Please tell me what to do."

Almost instantly, I heard a voice inside my head which said simply, "Stop drinking coffee."

I stopped drinking coffee. I have never touched another drop since that time. Immediately, I began to feel a lot better. The heartburn, indigestion, allergic reactions and irritability stopped. I became more calm and patient. In fact, you could even say that my improvement was dramatic.

My condition improved steadily for a few months, but I was still suffering from a large assortment of other miseries. I decided to ask for more help. Sitting up late that night, I again sent out the mental plea, "Please help me once more. Tell me what else I must do to feel better."

The answer came back at once, "Stop smoking."

I knew that the voice was right. I also knew that I was in for a struggle. I knew this because, like many other smokers, I had gone through the agony of withdrawal before, only to revert back to the habit. For someone like me, smoking was a severe addiction.

Nevertheless, I was determined. I made up my mind that this time I would kick the habit once and for all, and never again go back to smoking. So, for the next six weeks I suffered the tortures of withdrawal. During this time, I did smoke three or four cigarettes, but finally I triumphed. I knew I had won this battle — and war — permanently!

Having conquered the twin vices of coffee and cigarettes, both my physical and mental health responded positively. I had eliminated much physical distress and discomfort. I became mentally sharper, more objective and determined to continue my therapy. Emotionally, I discovered greater control returning along with optimism and self-confidence.

With the returning objectivity came the realization that a lot more improvements could be made in my general health. By conquering two vices, I suddenly became aware that I had many other bad habits that were contributing to other distressing symptoms of body, mind and emotions.

Through the practice of regular meditation, I began a systematic exploration of myself with the objective of

113

gradually eliminating all ingrained bad habits and sub-
stituting them with good habits. The principle was one of
selective denial. I had the experience and the awareness
to realize that you can't just stop all bad habits at once.
It must be a gradual process wherein good habits are
substituted for bad ones. It is really a process of unlearning conditioned patterns and replacing them with newly
learned patterns until the new pattern completely blocks
out the old one.

The next bad habit to be eliminated was the eating
of candy, ice cream and pastries. This was followed a
short time later by removing beef and pork from my diet.
I did however, continue to eat poultry and fish.

It was about this time that I met a most extraordinary man who introduced me to the concept of fasting
and cleansing the digestive tract. He explained to me how
the average person constantly ingests medicines, drugs,
pesticide residues, dangerous chemicals in drinking water,
hormones from animal meats and even airborne pollutants
into the body. He further explained that there was only
one way to eliminate these toxic materials from the body
and that was through fasting.

One way to fast, he said, was to drink only distilled
water with either lime or lemon juice and honey added.
The other way was to drink only fresh raw fruit and
vegetable juices. Only in this manner, he said, could dangerous chemicals be purged from the cell structure of the
body.

He went on to tell me how controlled, intelligent fasting can almost totally eliminate these poisons from the
system. He said these toxic ingredients accumulating in
the system over a lifetime, causes all manner of illnesses
which is seldom traced to the original cause.

Next, he explained how a lifetime of ignorant eating
habits can cause the walls of the colon to be lined with
an accumulation of unexpelled waste matter. This impac-
tion can result in an absorption into the system of very
harmful toxic materials which can cause all sorts of illnesses. He said that only an extended raw juice diet or
the regular practice of high enemas could eliminate and
prevent this condition permanently.

Thereafter, I began fasting regularly. I also arranged for a series of professionally administered high colonics (flushing of the colon) to cleanse my colon.

Needless to say, these measures called for a large measure of self-denial and self-discipline.

As a reward to myself for these denials, I began cultivating a taste for raw fruits, vegetables, nuts, cheeses and raw juices, all of which I suddenly found immensely satisfying.

These changes in my living patterns were accompanied by a growing self-assurance and self-discipline that manifested itself in every area of my life. My new feelings of health, confidence, and a cheerful attitude were not unnoticed by my associates. Everyone began to notice a new me that was emerging from the old.

As my overall health improved, so did my appearance. I bought new clothes to go with my new self-image. I thought new thoughts, positive thoughts. I gave up many acquaintances who did not share my enthusiasm for better health and a fuller life. I gave up organized religion after a time because it no longer offered anything to my continued growth. However, I did retain as many of the beautiful philosophies of my former religion as were applicable to my new-found understandings.

Two observations of great importance must be made here.

First, the more I gave up those old habits that had formerly possessed me and undermined my health, the freer I became. I suddenly began to realize how our bad habits hold us in servitude and slavery. Conversely, I began to realize the freedom and joy that accompanies self-discipline and self-control. I realized that when we 'give up' bad habits, we do not give up our freedom to enjoy life, we suddenly gain our freedom! This was one of the most important discoveries of my life.

Second, I became increasingly aware of my psychic senses and of the importance of developing these inherent capabilities. I became aware that everyone possessed them, but that few people developed them. I was rapidly learning that my welfare and progress were to a great extent attributable to my increasing psychic development. Through my unfolding psychic talents, I was led progressively from one level of achievement and attainment to another, from one realization to another. The better I felt, the more psychic I became, the more psychic I became, the better I felt.

There came a time, however, when I reached a danger point. In my enthusiasm for self-development, I was consumed with the ideal and desire of serving my fellow man. This took the form of almost total dedication to 'spiritual' matters, to the neglect of the 'physical'. During this period of time, I became imbalanced because of this one-sided approach. I had failed to take into consideration the obvious fact that no one can ignore the 'world' he lives in. I live in a physical planet, therefore while I am here, I must physically contend with those matters which require a physical approach and a physical solution.

It's all well and good to say, "God will take care of my every need as long as I am totally dedicated to the things of God." The only trouble is that this attitude generally ignores the fact that the physical world is just as much 'God' as the non-physical realms!

Once I realized the fallacy of this trap, I brought myself back down to Earth. I began to practice my present philosophy which requires considerable dexterity. It consists of keeping one's feet firmly planted upon the ground while one's head is gently prodding the clouds!

All of the above thoughts came flooding into my mind as I pondered a discourse delivered by the wise and renowned cosmic teacher, Djwhal Khul.

I was driving through the beautiful mountains of Western North Carolina when El Dorado overshadowed me (entered my aura). It was a crisp and sparkling clear autumn day. The leaves had all turned into a magnificent array of autumnal colors and every tree seemed to be vying with the other for my attention and approval. I approved of them all, for the panorama was truly breathtaking. Such a perfect day seldom comes more than once a year. Most of you will recall such a day when your spirits have literally been lifted up to the heavens by nature's combination of color, temperature, setting and splendor. I was driving alone (so I thought) enjoying this

116

rapport with the nature forces, when El Dorado's sudden presence further elevated my spirits into the indescribable realms of ecstasy. I had no recourse but to pull over to the side of the road at the next 'overlook' point and commune mentally. I could not risk driving those precarious mountain roads in such a state of bliss.

"How glad I am that you have chosen such a perfect time and place to come to me, El Dorado"!

"Because you were feeling so wonderful, so vibrant and alive, Joseph, I felt this to be the perfect time for you to receive an important discourse on health. With me today is the beautiful and beloved teacher of cosmic wisdom, Djwhal Khul. Many Earth channels have been privileged to receive communications from Djwahl Khul. His name is known, recognized and loved throughout our solar system and beyond. None are more active in spreading news of the Divine Plan and working with willing channels on Earth.

"Today we will provide you with a new and different experience, Joseph. I will remain within your auric force field while Djwhal Khul joins with us."

I closed my eyes so as to concentrate on the new experience of a second master entering my aura while the first master remained. Just as one cannot describe in words the presence of one master, the simultaneous presence of two is even more impossible of description.

"I have waited patiently for many years to communicate with you in this manner, Joseph. Along with El Dorado, I have worked closely with you through the power of mental suggestion, to help bring your health to a state of rejuvenation that would make you more receptive to higher teachings. El Dorado and I are both very pleased with your response to these suggestions and with the impressive progress you have shown in your palingenesis (rebirth, regeneration). We feel that it is time to point out to you how the Divine Plan is working to improve the health and the health consciousness of mankind.

"Since you have been the recipient of much assistance in regaining your own health, it might be appropriate to start there.

117

"The first step that you took to get well was to ask your doctor for help. When you judged correctly that he was unable or unwilling to properly diagnose your condition, you called out instinctively and intuitively to the unseen forces for guidance. In contrast to your experience with your doctor, you received an immediate helpful response. From that point onward, your health has gradually improved until today you are in excellent health.

"Unfortunately, most people live more or less the way that you once did. So long as they feel good, they give little attention to the matter of healthful living. As in your case, this complacency often leads to more bad habits that gradually undermine one's health.

"This happens very easily because of the often insidious manner in which one's good health begins to decline. It might be compared to the erosion of a riverbed. The wear is barely noticeable from day to day. Over a longer period of time, however, the wear takes it toll and can be easily measured. The eventual breakdown of health is rarely traced to the bad habits which actually produced this condition. Rather, the breakdown is usually diagnosed and treated symptomatically.

"The physical body is an awesomely complicated instrument. As El Dorado has said, it is a marvel of mechanical, chemical and electrical symmetry and artistry. It is very strong and durable. It is also very delicate and sensitive. In its strength and durability, it can withstand unbelievable abuse and neglect and still continue to function. In its delicacy and sensitivity, it reacts to the most subtle impressions in its environment, and can produce extraordinary discomfort from causes not sensed by the undeveloped conscious mind.

"The body's strength and durability come not from the physical instrument itself, but from the divine life force and mind power of the being using the body. The body's delicacy and sensitivity likewise come from the concurrent presence of the many finer bodies which El Dorado has already described to you. Thus, in essence, it is not the physical body itself which determines its destiny, but it is the quality of the occupying entity which controls its fate.

118

"We have seen many instances where the will to live has produced survival in a body that seemed incapable of supporting life. Likewise, we have seen many instances where 'death' seemed to result from the most trivial of causes.

"In your case, Joseph, you embarked early in life on a course of neglect of your precious body. You developed a taste for refined food products and a disdain for those natural foods which nature designed for the body's fuel. To further compound your error, you developed emotional and mental habits of a negative nature which led to an imbalance of your emotional, mental and subconscious bodies. Bear in mind that any imbalance of the finer bodies eventually manifests itself in physical illness as well.

"After an extended period of many years, the combined abuses of your physical, mental, emotional and astral bodies produced a crisis which forced you to take remedial action or 'die'.

"The quality of the remedial action which you successfully undertook, has produced your present state of good health. You are living proof of the fantastic resilience of the physical body. You are living proof of the power of the human mind and spirit in controlling one's destiny. You are living proof of the loving help given from beyond the physical vibrations of Earth!

"Your personal experience in rejuvenating yourself has taught you both the value and the necessity of good health habits.

"Since it is impossible to evolve into the fourth dimensional vibration unless one is in a state of good health, we must obviously accomplish a great deal in a short time in order to help prepare mankind. The most important message that we can possibly get across to mankind to accomplish this goal is "physician heal thyself"!

"In order to heal oneself, one has to 'know himself'. In order to know himself, one has to understand the different aspects or bodies that make up the total Self. Therefore the understanding required for one to embark upon the path of healing himself lies in his grasp of the non-physical as well as the physical parts of himself as described by El Dorado.

119

"In the final analysis, no doctor is going to heal you. The best that most doctors can do is sew up wounds, set fractured bones, stimulate faltered hearts, and otherwise 'patch up' abused bodies. They are ill-equipped indeed in knowledge and training concerning one's non-physical bodies, much less concerning the interaction of these bodies with the physical body. Most of them are equally lacking in knowledge about nutrition. Concerning the allopathic practice of dispensing drugs, almost all doctors are totally ignorant of the long range damage drugs render to the chemical balance of people's bodies.

"Indeed, some of the techniques devised to diagnose and treat patients, induce the very conditions they are designed to diagnose or cure. An example of this is the dangerous radiation scan technique which can precipitate a carcinoma when none exists, or can induce carcinomatosis when carcinoma presently exists.

"Further, where carcinoma is found to exist, the treatment is likely to consist of chemotherapy or cobalt radiation or surgery. Each of these procedures attacks the symptoms only, is dangerous and usually leads to permanent damage or death.

"The safest way to diagnose such a condition is through psychic methods which most doctors are unwilling or unprepared to accept or understand.

"Again, by way of example, the proper way to treat such a condition is nutritionally through a restoration of the body's natural chemical balance, and educationally through counseling, so that the patient will understand the interaction of the non-physical bodies that can produce malignancy (if this were the case). All too often, however, malignancies are caused by the introduction of drugs into the body to 'cure' other illnesses. The cause and effect relationship of most allopathic procedures is too seldom connected.

"This is in no way intended to be a mass indictment of the healing profession. There are too many dedicated and loving doctors, nurses and technicians for us to insinuate neglect on their parts. This is simply a statement of fact asserting that most doctors lack the knowledge to perform the healing function. There are many gifted healers in medicine, dentistry, osteopathy, homeopathy, chiropractic, etc. Unknown to many of them, however, is the fact that the greatest healing that they render to their patients is, in reality, the channeling of healing energies projected through them by physicians of the higher realms. In other words, many of their patients are getting well in spite of some of the procedures used to cure them.

"What you see happening in Earth today, and particularly in your country, the United States, is that the increasing cost of health care is placing it out of the reach of more and more people. This is for the good! As fewer and fewer people can afford the conventional kind of health care available, more and more people will seek to learn more about how to care for themselves. Physician, heal thyself! As more and more people learn to care for themselves, they must of necessity learn much more about themselves. You see them even now buying books to learn more about their own physiology, nutrition, sex, etc. You see them exploring various other avenues of understanding themselves such as meditation, awareness groups and inner development. You see a tremendous interest developing in the field of psychic or spiritual healing. You see more and more medical doctors themselves becoming aware of the limitations and shortcomings within their branch of the healing profession, and spreading out into the areas of natural healing such as acupuncture, chiropractic, nutrition, etc. There are even instances where the more open-minded doctors collaborate with psychics to increase their understanding and skills in treating their patients.

"All of this and much, much more is part of the Divine Plan to awaken mankind to a greater degree of health consciousness and to make healthful living an integral part of everyone's daily life.

"As many people have recognized, this century has witnessed the greatest acceleration of knowledge in the history of Earth. The reason for this onrush of information is to quickly prepare mankind for the great changes that will accompany the new vibration of the Great Cycle Orbit. Without this information, there would be little hope or opportunity for survival.

"Fortunately, the Divine Plan provides for sufficient knowledge to be presented to man of Earth in all areas of concern. If this knowledge is used, then survival will be assured.

"The field of health has been an area of the greatest concern and concentration for those of us who work in the higher dimensions. Within the framework of improving health and raising health consciousness, we have made great advances. There is no area of healing where we are not active. Our major efforts and concentration, however, must be focused on the area of psychic healing. There are many reasons for this.

"Psychic healing is the only kind of healing method available worldwide to all peoples. It is cheap and often given freely as an act of love by dedicated channels. It is the highest form of healing. Its use helps awaken in recipients the realization of higher forces working on their behalf. It requires the use of psychic abilities which we are trying to encourage. It is usually far more effective than the allopathy generally practiced by the medical profession, without producing the residual and often debilitating side effects caused by drugs.

"Psychic healing directs natural healing currents and vibrations to the underlying causes of illness rather than alleviating symptoms. At its best, psychic healing through competent channels permits doctors of far greater competency and knowledge than most Earth doctors to channel healing energies into the astral body, which in turn brings automatic balance to the physical body. Psychic healing might also make someone aware of past life influences which caused the diseased condition that is being treated, and thus encourage one to change a life style that is damaging to their health.

"All of this is not to imply that psychic healing is the immediate panacea for all of Earth's health problems. It is not. It is intended mainly to illustrate that we are emphasizing the psychic approach to healing as a very necessary adjunct to all of the other healing methods currently practiced in Earth.

"The best method of healing is that people begin to understand the causes of their illnesses and learn to heal themselves, Joseph, just as you have done. In our judgment, the best beginning is to educate people in the absolute importance of nutrition, hygiene and proper attitudes along with the necessity of proper fasting to cleanse their system.

"The time will probably come when customary methods are unavailable to the masses of people. At such a time, an understanding of psychic healing and self-healing may save thousands or millions of lives.

"We want the people of Earth to know that there are literally millions of their fellow human beings in the higher planes who are prepared to work through willing Earth channels. It would be of immeasurable benefit to the Divine Plan if large numbers from Earth would join with them in this great service to their fellow man.

"We are counting upon you, Joseph, to aid us in this respect. Our blessings, our love and our constant assistance and guidance are yours. We must leave you now for a while in order to attend to matters in other realms."

"I will do all I can to spread this knowledge, Djwhal Khul. I want to thank you for this discourse and to especially thank you for all the help you have given me to regain my health."

CHAPTER 9

The Unfolding Plan—Part VI

St. Germain Speaks On
The Psychic Explosion

"As you can see, Joseph, the Divine Plan is progressing. We come now to the final discourse before the most exciting and educational experience of your life.

"With me today is the beloved St. Germain, who is well known to knowledgeable students of the hierarchy, metaphysics and the occult. St. Germain will speak to you about the virtual explosion of psychic awareness that is occurring in Earth, and explain its significance in the Divine Plan."

The fact that I had anticipated El Dorado's presence was further evidence of my own increasing psychic capacities. I had also sensed that the discourses were to end soon and that some other exciting experiences lay ahead for me.

For the moment, though, St. Germain's presence within my aura was excitement enough. This beautiful master permeated my being with the most dynamic exaltation that I could possibly experience at this stage of my development.

"The enormous increase of interest in psychic matters, Joseph, represents the fulfillment of one of the most important objectives of the Divine Plan.

"Man is awakening!

"At times, progress may seem very slow, but in reality man is unfolding quite rapidly.

"No area of our concern is more important than stimulating man's inner awareness. We are using every legitimate means available to accomplish this goal. For unless man's psychic capacities begin to function, he will never comprehend the realities that govern his own being, his own future or his universe.

"You have been able to learn how this process works from your own awakening experience. First comes an interest in psychic matters brought about by personal psychic experiences. Then comes a period of reflection on the possible causes of the phenomena. This may be followed by the observation that such experiences are not unique, that they happen to everyone. Then, if you are following your true inner guidance, you may begin to develop an interest or an awareness in the non-physical forces that can produce such phenomena. Such an interest hopefully leads to greater spiritual awareness or to a search for more meaning to life.

"All the time that this interest is building, one's own Higher Self (Christ Self) is providing the impetus and incentive for even greater growth.

"As one's interest continues to grow, the universal law of attraction operates to bring one in contact with other like-minded individuals. This in turn can lead to a much greater awareness and can further heighten one's cosmic understanding.

"Look at what has happened in Earth in recent years as the growth of interest in psychic matters has accelerated. Interest in the psychic has gradually become more respectable. Whereas in the past, people were afraid to disclose their interest in these matters for fear of being labeled eccentric, people now openly discuss all manner of psychic experience.

"We have seen this gradual acceptance lead to university courses ranging from the study of brain wave behavior during altered states of consciousness, to the study of dreams, to courses in astrology. We have seen newpapers beginning to reflect this greater public interest by an increasing number of articles on psychic phenomena. There are now newspapers and magazines that are devoted exclusively to the psychic and to the occult. There have even been television series devoted to plots dealing with the psychic powers of the stars of the series.

"Many individuals who display unusual psychic capacities have received much publicity, motivating people further to look deeper into their own selves. Though we do not ordinarily mention names in these discourses, we feel that it may be relevant to give a specific example in this instance:

"Edgar Cayce.

"We mention Cayce for several reasons. First, he was a highly evolved soul who incarnated for the purpose of demonstrating psychic talents. Second, his life and his works were highly publicized and thoroughly documented. thereby giving 'scientific' credence to his accomplishments. Third, he was a beautiful human being, a truly spiritualized man whose life and efforts were dedicated to serving God and his fellow man. Fourth, his life and his example have resulted in countless thousands of individuals being awakened to the truth of reincarnation, psychic healing and an awareness of their innate psychic potential.

"In addition to the foregoing examples, we regularly read of prophecies by well known psychics published in daily newspapers.

"A number of books have appeared, containing messages channeled into Earth from other realms to help awaken man of Earth.

"Documented evidence of reincarnation has been widely publicized. There have been specific examples of children relating intimate details of a previous Earth incarnation from the recent past of which they could have had no knowledge in their present life.

"Psychic healers from all over Earth have cured many whom conventional doctors pronounced incurable.

"These and countless other examples could be given to illustrate the psychic explosion occurring in Earth.

"In spite of this proliferation, it does no good for people to experience or learn of these phenomena unless it stimulates them to search for an understanding of what these forces are, unless it produces an awareness within them that they possess the same potential abilities as anyone else, unless it awakens in them a desire to use their own inherent faculties to understand the nature of of their own selves.

"This we cannot accomplish for anyone. This they must do for themselves. It's like the ancient saying, 'You can lead a horse to water, but you can't make him drink'. We can produce all manner of occurrences to focus man's attention on the unseen world, but we cannot force him to use his God-given faculties to discern what is happening, or why.

"All too many people are deterred from investigating the psychic and the occult because of fear of the unknown. It is ignorance that produces fear. Ignorance is man's greatest enemy. Ignorance is the most loathsome culprit that walks the face of Earth. The fear that ignorance induces, enslaves more people than do tyrants. Fear indeed, enslaves all people who have not been freed from its bonds.

"There are powerful and greedy individuals and institutions in Earth who keep the masses ignorant in order to keep them subdued. This physical, mental and emotional bondage manifests itself in governments, in religions, in businesses, in so-called educational establishments, and in every other facet of life where people can be banded together to promote selfish interests.

"But God did not create mankind for slavery. Man enslaves himself by ignoring (ignorance *is* ignoring) and by refusing to recognize the reality of who and what he really is, a son of God momentarily occupying a physical body on a physical planet.

"Through the centuries, churchmen have sown tremendous fear in their followers concerning the great dangers of the occult. People have been warned of the jeopardy of delving into these unseen forces. They have been told that they are the work of the devil. If they are the work of the devil, Joseph, then there are a lot of us devils working devilishly hard to help save Earth and mankind from the folly of ignorance!

"There is no real danger involved when men of pure heart and pure intent delve into the unknown. It is a far greater danger that they do not! There are plenty of godly beings working to help man understand the mysteries of the unseen realms. These godly forces protect man from malevolent forces. It is only when man uses this knowledge for evil purposes that he need be concerned or afraid.

"Unfortunately, the term 'occult' still conjures to the minds of many, visions of demons, witches and boiling cauldrons, and evil alchemists hunched over smoking test tubes. Those who have these visions are those who have never made the effort to look into the subject. Of course, their very fears may have prevented them from making any kind of investigation. Whenever anything is shrouded in secrecy over a long period of time, an aura of mystery and fear develops. Then, those who are not privy to the secrets often imagine all kinds of fearful speculations.

"It was necessary through the centuries to keep many higher truths concealed from the masses in order to keep these truths from being profaned and misused. The preservation of these truths was entrusted to the initiates of secret societies. Occasionally, some who had been entrusted with the secrets would violate their sacred oaths and pervert the secrets to their own selfish end. The misuse and misdeeds of the few over a period of time, brought disrepute to the occult generally.

"But the time has now come in Earth history when all will be revealed; when all will be made known as it relates to Earth and man's experiences upon Earth. Thus, it is only natural and desirable that the psychic explosion should arrive and strip away the ignorance and fear that have for too long enslaved mankind.

"As in all of the other discourses, Joseph, many books could be written about the unseen forces and the necessity that man become aware of them. But wisdom is not born in a multiplicity of words. We believe that those who are sincere will discover in our brief discourses the seeds of truth that will find fertile ground in their minds, emotions and souls. Those who approach these revelations in a spirit of love and humility, will find in this paucity of words the power of God. They will find themselves frequently overcome with the awesome realization of the truth of these simple phrases. So be it. We love all mankind. We labor endlessly to prove it!"

"The truth of your words moves me to tears, St. Germain. If these truths affect others as they have affected me, then your message will be of great benefit to mankind."

CHAPTER 10

An Extraordinary Interlude—Part I

An Astral Journey To Venus

"That's right, Joseph, relax. Now I am going to enter your auric force field as I have on other occasions, only this time you will feel a much greater energy vibration."

"I have never in this life felt such an exhilaration, El Dorado, such a feeling of well-being. It is ecstasy and euphoria combining to transport my senses to a level that I did not know existed. I tingle all over. My mind, my emotions, my physical body are all enraptured. What is this sensation that is occurring to me?"

"What you are experiencing has been referred to many times as the quickening by the Holy Spirit. What is literally happening is that the speed of the electron movement within each atom of your physical, mental, emotional and astral or soul bodies has been increased or 'quickened' by the stimulation of the presence of my 'light body.' My light body is the operable vehicle or body that I use in the Christ realms of expression and manifestation. Wherever a Christed being manifests his or her presence, it affects the environment similarly by raising the vibration or frequency response of the surrounding atoms much like a tuning fork transfers its vibrations when struck. Since Christed beings are pure in their mental and emotional projections as well as purified in their souls, their presence imparts a feeling of great love and light that is perceived as you have described."

"This is the most wonderful feeling that I have ever experienced in this lifetime. Is this why you had me rent a room, so that I could experience and enjoy this feeling without interruption?"

"No, Joseph. I had you rent this room because I am going to take you on an astral journey, and it is important that your physical body remain undisturbed while we are gone."

"What's going to happen? Where are we going?"

"You will see soon enough what is going to happen as well as find out where we are going. Now I want you to remain perfectly still and concentrate on what I tell you to do. First, visualize that you are rising up slowly out of your physical body. As you visualize this, while keeping your eyes closed, picture yourself floating upward without the encumbrance of your body while I open the doorway between dimensions. You will feel a sudden lightness, followed by a tremendous surge of consciousness that will flood your mind. Now open your eyes."

"This is astonishing! I am outside my physical body! Here I am, standing suspended in midair, looking down at myself sitting there with my eyes closed. And I see that I am still in a body and also I seem to be connected in some way to my physical body. Is this my astral body that I am in?"

"Yes, your consciousness is now in your astral body. The connection that you sense between your astral body and your physical body is often referred to as the silver cord. This attachment will remain as long as your physical body is alive and functioning. No matter where your astral body travels in the universe, this connection is maintained. Should your physical body be threatened in any way while you are travelling astrally, you would be instantly rejoined to your physical body via this silver cord. While sleeping you have often had the experience of suddenly awakening with a strong jerk as if you were falling out of bed. This was caused by a very rapid return of your astral body into your physical body. A too sudden return causes a jolt to the physical body which almost invariably awakens one."

"I have had that experience many times. Why should it cause such a jolt?"

"Think of it like a rubber band. If you stretch a rubber band and slowly bring it back to its regular shape, nothing happens. But if you should release one end while it is stretched, it will snap back suddenly and cause a shock. Bear in mind that the astral body has substance and mass although it is much less dense than the physical body and is in a different dimension and vibration. In an average person, the astral body would weigh between one and two ounces. It is this substance and mass that produces the shock of impact when you return to the physical body too suddenly."

"Thank you for explaining that to me. I always wondered what caused that reaction.

"I feel so fantastic, so vibrantly alive, so alert and mentally sharp, so filled with curiosity and awe that I don't want to return to my physical body, El Dorado. I really wish that I didn't have to."

"You won't have to for a while, Joseph. When the time does come for you to return, however, remember that this is the great sacrifice of which it is spoken, 'greater love hath no man than one who lays down his life for his fellow man.' You have incarnated upon Earth, not out of karmic necessity, but to serve your fellow man. This is what it means to lay down one's life. It does not mean to lose one's life in a rescue attempt to save someone. It means to sacrifice one whole incarnation, one whole lifetime, to serve in the upliftment of mankind. It means sacrificing for a time the fruits of enjoyment which you have attained through evolution and effort. However, this sacrifice is not without its rewards. Such service to your fellow man results in great spiritual growth and attainment. One such lifetime, well spent, can advance a soul further than eons spent in a less challenging environment. Great growth is seldom accomplished without some degree of pain."

"If that is the case, I hope that the pain that I have suffered in this life is some indication of the growth that I have achieved."

"You have indeed achieved great growth in this life, my son Joseph, but even greater opportunities lie ahead for you."

"Is there any particular reason why you just called me your son?"

"Your question will be answered by your own consciousness within a few months."

"For the first time, El Dorado, I realize that I can see you. Before now, I have only been able to hear you and I could not visualize what you looked like. Seeing you, I cannot really describe you. You are at once radiant and glorious. Just standing here in your light and in your aura fills me with the most perfect peace, contentment, joy and fulfillment that I have ever known."

"You have known it, Joseph, you just don't remember it. Come, take my hand. We have much to do and see in the next few hours. Forget about time, however. In the dimensions through which we will be traveling, we will not be limited by a few hours of three dimensional Earth time. For what you are about to see and experience, kings would gladly give their kingdoms, but such a trip cannot be paid for in money. It can only be paid for in sacrifice and service, and you have paid the price.

"Remember, we are not subject to the limitations of Earth or the third dimension. Wherever I take you, we can be there instantly. All things, all beings throughout the Universe are an integral part of the One Great Whole. All things are therefore attached in a way that could be roughly compared to the silver cord that connects your astral body to your physical body. Later you will be given a discourse on the unity of all matter and antimatter which will further explain this mystery.

"To transport ourselves to the farthest reaches of the Infiniverse (i.e., all universes combined), all we have to do is attach ourselves to our point of destination by our thought. Then, just as the silver cord can bring you back to your Earthly physical body instantly or in a leisurely manner, you can exercise your thought power to transport yourself to any destination in the same manner. The first stop on our itinerary will be that nearest and beautiful sister planet of Earth, Venus. Now you must remember, Joseph, you will not be viewing things on this journey through your three dimensional eyes, therefore things may appear different than you have conceived them to be in your mortal mind. For example, if you were viewing Venus from Earth, you could not even see the surface of the planet because of the dense atmosphere. And if you could see through this very thick vapor, you would only view what appears to be a hot and hostile environment laced with smoke holes and lava. Bear in mind that man is not manifested in the same vibration upon Venus as he is upon Earth. What you will be seeing is man manifested in the fourth dimensional vibration of Venus.

"We will make our journey rapidly but not instantly. This will afford you the opportunity of viewing in perspective the marvelous construction and the balanced perfection of our solar system. One cannot help but compare our solar system to a gigantic, macrocosmic atom. Indeed, that is exactly what it is. Everything that is within our solar system is unified within one large force field that embraces the entire solar system.

"As we approach Venus, we will slowly orbit the planet at a low altitude so that you can discern various features of the topography and study the orientation of the cities and the rural terrain. You will note the total absence of atmospheric pollution within the fourth dimension. The energy sources of Venus are very advanced by Earth concepts and the industries are clean. Ecologically, the Venusians (or Hesperians as they are also known) are in perfect rapport with their environment. Note the symmetry and logic with which the cities are laid out. They conform to the natural lines of magnetic force which reticulate the planet. This enables the Hesperians to readily convert and utilize inherent planetary energy forces for their everyday use with very little effort and expenditure. Notice the marvelous balance between the developed areas and the areas that are in their natural state. Notice also the great beauty that exists everywhere. In the fourth dimensional plane of Venus, man lives in perfect rapport with the elemental beings or nature forces. Through this enlightened cooperation, the elemental beings never cease in their efforts to please man.

"Let's stand on a sidewalk in one of these beautiful cities and talk to one of the inhabitants. Of course you do not need to be concerned about language. As you already know, communication is mind to mind, the same as between us. Are you ready?"

"Yes, I am ready and eager."

"This looks like a good spot. We'll just stand here. You engage the first passerby in conversation and I will remain silent unless spoken to. Neither of us can be seen in the conventional sense by the physical eye, because you are manifesting in an astral body and I am manifesting in an Etheric or Christ body. However, you will soon discover that the vision of the Hesperians is not limited to their physical eyes as it is with the people of Earth."

As we stood watching, it was fascinating to observe the pedestrians on the opposite sidewalk (our side was temporarily vacant). The first thing that registered in my mind was everyone's evident good health and vibrancy. The next thing I observed was the physical beauty of everyone. Then I noticed the cordiality that was exchanged between passersby in both obvious and subtle ways. It felt really good, even exalting, to see people relate to each other with such love and respect.

While I was thinking these thoughts and making these observations, I became aware that a man was approaching us on our side of the street. As he came closer, it seemed to me that he was looking at us as if he knew we were there. As he reached us, I spoke to him mentally.

"Hello, I am Joseph Whitfield! I have come from Planet Earth in my astral body with my friend, El Dorado, and I would like to talk to you."

"Greetings and blessings my brother Joseph. Welcome to Venus. How may I enhance your visit and that of the beautiful Christ, El Dorado, to this planet?"

"How did you know that El Dorado is a christ?"

"We of Hesper (Venus) develop our higher spiritual faculties (psychic senses) from an early age, and therefore we readily perceive that which remains hidden to men of Earth. My name is Velsin. I sensed that I would be meeting someone from Earth today. It is my added privilege and joy to also meet El Dorado whose name is known throughout the solar system and beyond."

"Thank you, Velsin, for your gracious welcome. I have brought Joseph to Venus as part of his indoctrination into the realities of human life as it expresses in various dimensions and planets of our solar system. Joseph is soon to assume great responsibilities in the administration of the Divine Plan as it unfolds upon Earth. By observing life styles and human development upon the more advanced planets, he may be able to help influence the progress and direction of the evolution of Earth.

"You are known to me, Velsin, for the reputation that you have achieved in your position as energy coordinator for the planet. When one serves his fellow man as well as you have, his fame soon spreads far and wide."

"Thank you for your gracious comments, El Dorado."

"I too, am very interested in energy sources, Velsin. The Earth is undergoing a so-called energy crisis at this time and scientists are searching for alternative sources for generating energy that are both economical and conserve our natural resources. What is your primary energy source on Venus?"

"Joseph, we long ago recognized that energy is limitless throughout the universe. For example, as your Earth scientists have already discovered, every atom has locked within itself a portion of this limitless energy supply. Wherever life manifests itself in embodiment as a living being, the force inherent within each atom is magnified within the force field of that living being. Furthermore, this very living being sets up a continuous energy flow from the etheric antimatter body to the physical matter body, as long as life is sustained in the physical embodiment. In applying this knowledge to the realization that our planet was a living being, we eventually learned how to tap and harness that energy flow for the benefit of everyone upon the planet. You can note that all of our cities and developments are laid out in precise patterns. These patterns conform to the natural lines of force within Venus. These lines of force are produced by the flow of life force that I have described."

"Would you show me how to tap that energy flow, Velsin?"

"Yes, Joseph, I will show you. But you must guard this knowledge very carefully. If those with vested interests on Earth were to learn of these methods, then mankind might not benefit adequately from the knowledge. The vested interests might selfishly apply these methods for their own gain rather than for the public welfare. You see, this system of energy production provides a limitless supply at what amounts to negligible costs per capita. The equipment required is very long-lasting and dependable. I would imagine that the vested interests upon Earth would be tempted to use our methods without giving the public the benefit of the cost differential. They would thereby vastly and unjustly enrich themselves to the detriment of mankind on Earth."

"You are very perceptive in your analysis, Veslin. If this secret were to get into the wrong hands, a vast concentration of wealth would be placed at the disposal of those who could thereby control the planet for their own selfish ends. We already have the unfortunate example of a small group of greedy and arrogant men disrupting the Earth's economy by raising the price of oil to extortionate levels. This has caused the greatest suffering among those who are least able to help themselves. Whatever wealth accrues by adopting this method on Earth will be used to benefit all and to impoverish none.

I thank you for entrusting this formula to me. I will guard it with my life."

At this point El Dorado and I took our leave, thanking Velsin for his courtesies and expressing our desire to visit him again. El Dorado then took me on a quick tour of the city. The purpose of this tour was to acquaint me first hand with the life style of its citizens, their method of governing, their state of spiritual, social and technological development, and perhaps most of all to observe the loving relationship linking all of the inhabitants. One could not possibly visit Venus without realizing that it was a paradise. One would be left with the compelling impression that this is what life should be like on Earth.

"Well, El Dorado, I am certainly leaving Venus with reluctance. I can say with complete sincerity that I would gladly stay here for a lifetime. Where are we going next?"

CHAPTER 11

An Extraordinary Interlude—Part II

A Visit To Saturn
A Meeting With The
Spiritual Hierarchal Board

"Our next stop will be planet Saturn. There are things to be seen and learned there that will give you a deep insight into the spiritual government of our solar system as well as give you an idea of life upon the other planets of our solar system and beyond.

"Saturn is the fourth dimension headquarters of our spiritual leaders who are known as the Saturnian Council or the Council of Seven. It is from the fourth dimensional level of Saturn that the council governs the spiritual affairs that affect the physical levels of expression on all of the sister planets within the solar system. This council is our highest ruling body. It consists of seven master directors or chohans, who are under the guidance of the archangels of our solar system.

"There are seven steps that man must complete, or master, as he evolves through the physical, three dimensional experience into the fourth dimensional, cosmic conscious level of being. Each of these steps is under the spiritual direction and guidance of one of the chohans.

"I have been in mental communication with the Saturnian Council, Joseph. They are presently meeting on Saturn and they have given their permission for you to meet with them while on this special journey. This is an unusual honor that is being granted to you. The critical state of Earth's evolution requires that someone from Earth learn the truth about our spiritual hierarchy and present this information on Earth. The meeting that we will be attending is being presided over by Lord Michael, the Archangel of the first ray, spiritual head of our solar system."

While El Dorado was briefly explaining the Saturnian Council to me we were making our transit from Venus directly to Saturn. As we approached Saturn, I could not help exclaiming to El Dorado about the magnificent view.

"What a spectacularly beautiful sight! Saturn is like an exquisite and resplendent jewel with its delicate rings encircling it. It is so ethereally engrossing that I could just stop here and look at it for a long time. What is the purpose of the rings?"

"Among other things, Joseph, the rings act as an armature providing magnetic protection for the planet. Their rotation around Saturn sets up a unique force field

145

which automatically repels any negative entity from approaching within the thought atmosphere of Saturn. As the seat of spiritual government in the solar system, Saturn is off-limits to beings of evil intent."

"What a tremendous feeling of exhilaration as we enter the force field, El Dorado. I feel so much love, so much joy and happiness. It's like giant magnets are reaching within me and pulling these feelings out. I'm intoxicated with love and well-being."

"The force field has that reaction on entities of good will, Joseph. As we did with Venus, we'll orbit Saturn slowly so that you can get a general idea of its makeup and characteristics."

As we orbited the planet from several different directions so that I could get an impression of the topography, I noticed one large area that was entirely different from all the rest.

"What is that unusual area down there El Dorado? It looks totally unlike any other part of the planet. It looks like a composite of many different planets. Even the structures are extremely varied and uniquely styled."

"I will tell you later, Joseph, or rather you will see for yourself. That will be our second stop. First, we will meet with the Saturnian Council. Here we are. See that huge iridescent building that is shaped like a pyramid with a gold capstone?"

"Yes! What an unusual structure. Iridescent is a perfect word to describe it. Each of the four sides looks like mother-of-pearl, alternating between the purest soft-white glow and delicate pastel rainbow hues, as we move around it. And the contrast provided by the four huge golden corners that connect the capstone to the base, produces a stunning effect. The building gives me the feeling that it is alive."

"That building is the holiest of temples, Joseph. Its construction is the most perfect that man, in union with Divine Spirit, can devise. The craftsmanship that created it was the finest, the most skilled and dedicated that could be found within the entire solar system. The materials used in its construction are unmatched anywhere in quality, purity and durability. The building is designed to last as long as required. Its very shape provides a force field that preserves everything within in a state of perfection. Every aspect, down to the minutest detail is as perfect as could be created up to the time of its completion thousands of years ago. Nothing within it is without meaning or purpose, as you will see.

"Inside the doorway to the great temple is a guardian spirit who has been vested with Divine authority by the Archangels to insure that no entity gain access without permission. Entry is restricted to those who have attained the status of Christhood."

"How, then, am I to be permitted entry, El Dorado?"

"Beyond the veil of your mortal memory, Joseph, there was a lifetime in which you were glorified by the ascendency into the Christhood. You must have begun to realize by now, that there are eons of experience within your soul memory pattern that are presently hidden from your mortal conscious mind. That you have chosen to temporarily sacrifice that memory in service to your fellow man in no way robs you of certain privileges which accrue to your attainment. Come, we will now enter the temple."

"Welcome, blessed and beloved children of the Father-Mother Creator. You are awaited in the inner temple of the Most High by Lord Michael and the Seven Masters. We greet you in love and we salute the Divine Life Force within you," spoke the guardian spirit.

"We love, recognize and salute the Divinity within you, oh blessed guardian of the holy temple, and we thank you for the protection that you provide for these sacred precincts," replied El Dorado.

"Come this way, Joseph. There is no entry to the inner temple except by invitation and summons of the Saturnian Council. Let us stand here a moment on this golden slab and we will presently be transported by teleportation into the presence of the Council. This manner of entry into the inner temple of the Most High, absolutely insures that no one can enter unauthorized.

El Dorado and I stood on the golden slab for barely an instant before I suddenly realized that we were in the presence of Lord Michael and the Seven Masters within the inner temple. This was the most unusual of experiences. There was absolutely no consciousness of the teleportation process. It was simply a matter of being one place one instant and another place an instant later, without being aware of a lapse of time or of any movement. Lord Michael, the Archangel, spoke to us.

"Beloved El Dorado and Joseph. Your presence fills us with joy. We embrace you with Divine Love and bid you sit with this council. Your presence here is of epochal significance for the planet Earth."

"Thank you Blessed Michael for your warm welcome to Joseph and me. Thank you also, my brothers of the Council of Seven, for inviting us to meet with you on this special occasion."

"Joseph, it is appropriate that the members of the Council introduce themselves to you individually and briefly describe their spiritual function within the Council. As you already know, I am Archangel of the first ray. As such, I have primary responsibilities for the spiritual evolution of mankind within this solar system."

"In the Christ realms of our solar system, Joseph, I am known as El Morya. As El Dorado has already told you, there are seven steps that man must complete, or master, when he chooses to evolve within this solar system. Successful completion of these evolutionary steps is climaxed by being annointed into the Christhood. Each of these steps is known as a ray of life. Each ray of life has a master director, or chohan, on the Christ level. Within our solar system, I am chohan of the first step, or ray of life, which concerns itself with the spiritual function of power and will. It is my duty and privilege in this position to use the power of the word to implement the will of Spirit. Lord Michael is my guide and teacher on the Archangelic level."

"Joseph, I am the chohan of the second ray of life. I met with you under El Dorado's guidance to deliver the discourse on Atlantis, telling you of coming changes in our solar system and life on other planets. Now you are actually seeing for yourself that life does indeed exist on Earth's sister planets. I am known in this council as Kut Humi, but like everyone else here, I have many identities on many levels. The second ray is called the intellectual ray, and concerns itself with wisdom and understanding and mental health and balance. Through the second ray, one uses the intellectual processes to gain understanding of divine laws and learns to use wisdom in applying them. The Archangel Jophiel guides me in my second ray responsibilities. We are very glad to have you meet with us and have you see how the spiritual affairs of mankind are actually administered within our solar system. Man of Earth has such erroneous concepts concerning God and the hereafter. I will continue to be working very closely with you, Joseph."

"I am called Lanto, Joseph. I am chohan of the third ray, the ray of love, which incorporates the heart or feeling nature of man as he expresses the will of the first ray to do the will of his own God Self, as well as the intellect of the second ray that gives understanding in applying divine laws. You would know of me as Paul the Venetian or Paolo Caliari of Verona, incarnated in Italy in the sixteenth century. Chamuel, the Archangel, heads the third ray of our solar system and guides me in my third ray responsibilities. This council actively works with the light workers of Earth, though most are not even consciously aware of us. If all light workers could share the experience that you are now having, Joseph, it would surely inspire them in their efforts to implement the Divine Plan. Since it is impossible for all of them to make this journey, you must share this experience with as many as you can. We welcome you into our midst, and stand behind you in all of your efforts."

"Greetings, Joseph! As Pythagoras, I am remembered for introducing the Pythagorean mathematical theory to Earth in the sixth century B. C. In this honored council, I am known as Serapis Bey, chohan of the fourth ray of cohesion or crystallization. I am sometimes humorously referred to by my fellow chohans as number four, or the square, or the middleman or halfway Bey. Others refer to me both humorously and seriously as the crystal man. The fourth ray represents a balancing of matter with antimatter, flesh with fantasy, physical with metaphysical, three dimensional with four dimensional. To master this step, one must utilize the spiritual faculties to give fullness of meaning and understanding to the physical and intellectual processes. It requires the capacity to bridge dimensions, the third to the fourth dimension. It is the final step that is to be mastered while still manifested in a physical body. The Archangel Gabriel is my guide in fourth ray evolvements. I am very glad that you are here, Joseph. Man of Earth can certainly use the knowledge that you will be able to introduce upon your return, if he will but listen. I will soon deliver to you a discourse of the greatest importance concerning the communication factor of the universe. This discourse will help you crystallize your understanding of the unity of matter and antimatter. Look for me!"

"Well, Joseph, you could remember me as Plato. You were one of my students. Later, when I was known as Paul the Apostle, you also had an Earth incarnation that brought us together again. Through the ages of Earth history, many of us have worked together in helping to unfold the Divine Plan, though we seldom were aware of it while physically incarnated! Here, I am known as Hilarion, chohan of the fifth ray. It was as Hilarion that I came to you and delivered the discourse on UFO's. Fifth ray activity involves integration, healing, cooperation and unification. On the physical dimensions, it involves using the five senses to the highest degree to develop one's psychic powers. Through the development of psychic powers, one establishes his unity with, and understanding of all other realms, dimensions and beings. By means of this unity, one then possesses the tools to bring himself into perfect balance and harmony. Raphael, the Archangel, is my fifth ray guide, guardian and teacher. My fondest welcome to you, my brother."

"You knew me, Joseph, as the disciple Matthias. I was also known as Appolonius of Tyana, Count Rakoczi (Comte St. Germain) and Christopher Columbus, among other Earth personalities. Welcome to our council. I am known now in this function as St. Germain. This is the identity that I used while delivering my discourse to you concerning the psychic and the occult. I am chohan of the sixth ray of life, the ray of transmutation. This ray provides the purification and the balance required in order to synthesize all opposite aspects within yourself so that you may be completely solidified within your own consciousness. This means that in your dedication to the God Force, Man and God within you are equally balanced, as well as male and female, matter and antimatter, and conscious-subconscious.

"While on Earth as Christopher Columbus, it was my function to 'discover' America. This was an integral part of the unfolding Divine Plan. Much of my present attention is therefore being directed toward the United States as it re-creates its Atlantean development in order to rectify past errors, and evolve into the New Age of fourth dimension consciousness. This means that the mistakes that were made in Atlantis now have to be recognized and corrected. If all goes as planned, the United States will continue to provide the main focal point for leading the rest of Earth into the Aquarian Age of love and understanding. Otherwise, the focus will be switched to Brazil.

"Zadkiel is my Archangelic counterpart. I echo Serapis Bey's sentiment: I am very glad that you are here. Earth can certainly use the knowledge that you will be able to impart upon your return. May your every effort be blessed with success."

"My beloved Joseph, what a joy to be together again, and to be completing this plan in which we have worked for so many eons. Little did you realize in your conscious mind when you were receiving my discourse, that you have had Earthly incarnations that parallelled some of mine. You and I have been together many times in implementing the Divine Plan upon Earth. We are together again now. I am Sananda, chohan of the seventh ray of life, which is the final step in man's evolution within this solar system. This step marks the completion of the evolutionary process that begins when man's spirit first assumes a three dimensional physical body form. In the seventh ray one recognizes the divine life force that exists within all of creation, and relates to this divine life force with love and peace and understanding. One recognizes that the divine life force is God, expressed in countless myriads of individualized forms, and one further recognizes the wholeness of which everything is a part.

"Earth is in the throes of rending the seventh veil. The effect of this rending is to release man of Earth from his ignorance so that he may choose among his options for future evolution. Releasing man from his ignorance has caused horrendous repercussions as soul patterns are released from his subconscious mind so he can recognize and rectify them. It is at this crucial time that mankind upon Earth needs to have truth and enlightment so that he can make intelligent choices concerning immediate evolutionary opportunities in this solar system.

"It falls upon you, Joseph, to play a key role in bringing enlightenment to your fellow man. The primary purpose of this journey is to prepare you further for that role. You are operating primarily upon the seventh ray principle in your present incarnation. The Archangel Uriel, who guides me in seventh ray functions, is also guiding you in the manifestation and expression of the divine love principle that this ray teaches. We all therefore embrace you with all of the divine love, life, light, truth, peace and joy that one Christ can impart to another. We bless you and are confident that you will fulfill the role that is yours to perform.

"Would you speak to us, Joseph?"

"I will let my heart speak to you, beloved masters, for I am too overwhelmed and overawed from this experience to be coherent. I feel such a deep love for each of you, that it brings tears of joy to my eyes. The love which you project to me is so all-encompassing that it almost renders me speechless. If being a Christ means to continuously feel and express such intense love, then surely all of mankind would aspire to the Christhood if they but knew this.

"As you introduced yourselves, I recognized each of you from deep within myself. I sensed the tremendous sacrifices that each of you have made in attaining your present state of evolution. Furthermore, I realized that it was these very sacrifices that have made you so wise, so compassionate and so loving towards all mankind. As each of you spoke, it filled me with desire to emulate you. I silently resolved to redouble my efforts to serve the Divine Plan. With leaders such as you guiding and directing us, I have total confidence that God's Plan for man of Earth will succeed. I can only add my humble thanks and gratitude for all of your help. I pledge to each of you my eternal love and service."

"Thank you for your pledge, Joseph. I speak for the chohans, as well as for myself as Michael, Archangel of the first ray, when I pledge to you our love and service in return. El Dorado has already told you that full aid and assistance is available at all times to those who do their share and who ask for help. This is Universal Law and it will always apply. Have you any questions that you wish to ask at this time?"

"Blessed Michael, I would like to ask about the spiritual Hierarchy of this solar system. What is it and how does it work?"

"The spiritual Hierarchy of this solar system consists of masters, teachers, disciples and aspirants of spiritual knowledge and understanding who are dedicated to performing Spirit's will in all matters. The level of consciousness and attainment of these individuals draws them together through the Universal Law of attraction to work together on the Divine Plan. The organization thus created is known as the spiritual Hierarchy. In this Hierarchy, or system of government, there is a group consisting only of masters which is referred to as the Hierarchal Board. This group of masters is also variously known as the White Brotherhood, the Ascended Masters Council and the White Lodge. The term 'white' used in this context is not to be misconstrued. The spiritual Hierarchy works unlike any system of government known upon Earth. Members of the Hierarchal Board are motivated and activated solely by the Will of the Father-Mother-Creator-God Principle. The level of spiritual development and understanding of Hierarchal Board members enables them to be attuned to the Will of Spirit from within their own being. Accordingly, they are constantly aware of how to fulfill the next step in their own ongoing evolution as it relates to the overall Divine Plan.

"Have you any further questions, Joseph?"

"There are many questions that are in my mind, Blessed Michael, but I would not presume to take this Council's valuable time to answer questions that might be inappropriate. I would simply ask that you read my heart and mind and give me whatever answers and information required at this time."

"You demonstrate deep humility and perception, Joseph. I will tell you what you need to know. The answer to many, many questions has already been given to Earth through Hierarchal channels on every continent. You are already aware of this through your own studies. Continue to seek out these channels and study those messages to which you are guided. Should you need knowledge not available through these sources, then go within yourself and ask of your own Higher Self revelation of that which you seek. Seek and you will always find. This is the Law. For now, El Dorado still has much to reveal to you on this journey.

"Come, Joseph, and sit in this chair while we give you our blessing to take back to that planet which represents the heart of our solar system. May the love in our hearts and throughout the Christ and Angelic realms envelop you. May all who read your words or hear your voice or touch you in any way be uplifted. May the truth of your testimony evoke in all men of Earth a recognition of the Divine Plan of God. So be it. It is done. Go now in peace and with the sure knowledge of our assistance in all matters."

As I sat in a special gold chair overhung by a magnificent crystal, the chohans and Lord Michael formed a circle around me, each placing his left hand upon my head and his right hand upon the shoulder of the person to his right, forming a closed wheel with me as the axle. As I was thus energized and unified in this circle of light and love, my consciousness and awareness was momentarily one with Universal Mind—an experience that no mortal can ever forget or surpass.

As El Dorado and I were teleported out of the inner temple, I felt totally overjoyed with the magnitude of my experience. If I had been in my mortal, physical embodiment, I would probably have felt somewhat intoxicated. As it was, my mind was sharp and clear and I was eagerly anticipating my next experience.

"Where to next, El Dorado?"

"Do you remember commenting on how unusual the surrounding area looks?"

"Yes."

"This is our next destination."

"What is it?"

"It is just what it appears to be, Joseph. You will note that the great temple lies in the geographical center of this area that comprises the varied topography. What you

154

see here is the Saturnian equivalent of the United Nations and a world's fair exposition."

"It sounds and looks fascinating!"

"This is probably the most fascinating spot of the physical dimensions of our solar system. What you see here is a representation of life upon every planet of the solar system. What was most obvious to your eye when we first approached this area was the seeming incongruity of the terrain. Let me assure you, there is nothing more congruent in the entire physical solar system than what you see represented here. Every planet has been allotted a large area to develop. Within the allotted area of each planet you will find more differences than just the terrain. You will find a true depiction of the architecture as reflected in the houses and buildings. You will find that the plant and animal life is accurately portrayed; in some instances by actual life forms and in other instances by simulated forms. There is a unique energy force field here that permits various life forms from the different planets to coexist within the same general area. Nowhere else in the entire solar system is this possible. This force field emanates from, and is maintained by the apparatus of the Hierarchal Board within the great temple. The technology of all planets except Earth permits the inhabitants of other planets to temporarily change or alter the dimension in which they are manifested. However, in no instance except this is the alteration allowed to be permanent.

"An example of a temporary alteration of dimensional vibration would be the interplanetary spacecraft that sometimes make themselves visible in Earth's atmosphere. Such vibrational change is always of relatively short duration. It would be dangerous for non-Earth inhabitants to remain too long in a vibration as low as the present vibration of Earth. A point would be reached when the craft and its occupants would become entrapped in the lower vibration and would be unable to leave. It is only by special dispensation that this exception is permitted on Saturn. I will tell you why.

"The whole purpose for all of the varied forms of physical life that exist throughout the Universe is to allow man to experience all that he requires in his eternal living and ongoing, in order to reach that point of spir-

155

itual evolution when he can progress to Christhood and beyond. If man were allowed to move freely from one physical dimension to another before his level of consciousness was spiritually developed, we would find many attempting to escape the karmic conditions created by their errors. Of course, no one can escape the karma of their actions. Moreover, free movement through physical dimensions by spiritually immature men would result in a chaotic imbalance and disharmony. This, Spirit does not permit.

"So, because of special dispensation, life forms of the various planets are permitted to live and manifest themselves side by side in this unique environment. People from the different planets live fairly normal lives here. The length of their stay depends upon many factors. However, I am sure that anyone that you speak to will tell you that this is the most exciting, fulfilling and rewarding experience of their present incarnation."

"I'm sure that I would find it tremendously thrilling to be able to stay here, El Dorado!"

"No one of Earth stays here at this time, Joseph. The area set aside for Earth is peopled by simulated human beings such as you find in your Disneyland or Disney World. It will be a joyful day when man of Earth can again take his rigthful place among the men of his sister planets.

"No effort has been spared to depict life as realistically as possible. The life styles, cultures, social life, spiritual life, forms of work, opportunities for education and development, recreation, transportation, communication, technology, planetary history, planetary karma, entertainment, geography and more are all found in each area.

"There is an exchange program whereby one spends a given time in planetary areas other than one's own. It is the high point of one's stay here when one begins these visits outside of their own area. As you can see, human beings do not always look the same on every planet. Can you imagine the shock of someone from Earth suddenly finding himself on Uranus? Without advanced preparation, it would surely be traumatic. Because of the advanced understanding of those who come here, however, the exchange program produces pleasure instead of trauma.

"It often happens that one meets a person from another planet whom one has known in previous life episodes. This is particularly exciting and stimulating. The more diverse their appearances and planetary lifestyle, the more interesting the encounter."

"This is true education in the cosmic sense, El Dorado. I would like to see something like this reproduced on Earth to educate my fellow man to the realities of eternal living. It would certainly be the most popular attraction upon Earth!"

"No such undertaking would be possible at the present time, Joseph. It would require the cooperation of your brothers from the other planets. Perhaps in the not too distant future, when Earth vibrations are higher and when Earthman has had an opportunity to adjust to the facts of extraterrestrial human existence within the solar system, it might be feasible to begin such a project.

"Now here we are at the spaceport. As you can see, there are interplanetary spacecraft from every planet. Of course, those from Earth over there are over 26,000 years old. Hopefully, we will have some updated versions in the not too distant future. Observe the great variety of designs, shapes and sizes. The craft shaped like a boomerang are from Mars. The cigar shaped ones are from Venus. The ones shaped like flying saucers come from city size mother ships from Jupiter. Each planet has a number of different designs reflecting different uses and technologies based upon their own particular state of development. You might compare their variety to the aircraft of Earth, where you have everything from single engine propeller driven two-passenger pleasure craft, to supersonic jet transports.

"This section of the spaceport is reserved for craft arriving from outside of our solar system."

"Wouldn't Earth scientists be astounded at this, El Dorado? In the limitations of their present thinking, they think in terms of hundreds of years for travel between our solar system and the closest planet outside of our solar system. If only they could be made to realize that these limitations exist only in their minds."

"Breakthroughs will come soon, Joseph. The time is rapidly approaching when interplanetary spacecraft will have to land on Earth and make official contact with some of Earth's leaders. When this takes place, man of Earth will simply have to face reality and adjust his thinking accordingly. If Earth's scientists and engineers are willing and cooperative, they will be given many keys and clues to aid them in their development."

"Is there much contact with life outside of our solar system, El Dorado?"

"Yes, there is considerable contact. Life exists throughout all of creation. All forms of life. Life exists also in realms which are still invisible to you. There are other planets in this solar system which are not visible to those incarnated upon the visible planets. Does this shock you? Do not let it, for is it not said, 'in my Father's house there are many mansions!' Remember, all of creation is unified, despite appearances to the contrary.

"It is necessary for communication to exist between our solar system and other systems, other galaxies, other universes beyond your mortal ability to comprehend. Those from other systems who wish to expand their incarnational experiences to our particular system, frequently visit here before incarnating. This area of Saturn provides them with a showcase, so to speak, of life in our solar system. Here they can study the life forms available to them and decide if Spirit's needs for them will be met by experiencing life in our solar system. Similar showcases exist elsewhere depicting life in other parts of our galaxy and beyond."

"I would assume from what I have learned so far, El Dorado, that the Spiritual Hierarchy extends beyond our solar system and that our solar system Hierarchy is but a small part of a much greater whole."

"You assume correctly, Joseph. The Spiritual Hierarchy is all-encompassing and interconnected by Universal Mind to all who are attuned to it."

"What you are saying, in effect, is that all who are attuned to Universal Mind, and who have reached a state of cosmic consciousness, are more or less automatically a part of the Spiritual Hierarchy. It that right?"

"That is exactly right. To the extent that one is in harmony with the Divine Life Force that exists within one's self, that exists within all creation, within every atom, then to this extent will one be attuned to Universal Mind. When this harmony or state of attunement reaches a point where one is totally aware that he is one with Universal Mind, that is when one knows that 'the Father and I are One'. This is precisely what Jesus and other great masters have taught, but which has been so misunderstood and misconstrued by many of their followers. To reach that point of consciousness is to be filled with the desire to do the will of Spirit. All who do the will of Spirit with full consciousness and knowledge are part of the Spiritual Hierarchy."

"It is really so very beautiful and so simple. Why is it that we men of Earth find it so difficult to grasp?"

"Men become so wrapped up in their sophistication and intellectual pride that they become unable, Joseph, to turn their minds and their hearts to the simple, eternal, prevailing truths of Divine Law. The intellect then becomes like a drug, addicting them to the pursuits of itself. The feelings become dulled, then ignored. In such an atmosphere, the still small voice from within can scarcely be heard.

"However, events are now taking place upon Earth that are forcing more and more to listen. Many are reaching the point of realizing that man is not capable alone of solving the manifold problems that he has caused. What seem to be solutions to problems often turn out to produce greater problems. The very magnitude and complexity of Earth's problems must eventually force mankind to turn to Universal Law for solutions."

"How can we hasten this process, El Dorado?"

"By mass education and communication, Joseph. By educating mankind to the reality of intelligent life beyond Earth that is ready and capable of giving assistance and guidance.

"Man of Earth cannot be forced to accept what is given, but as the 'vibrations' of Earth continue to rise, you will find more and more people becoming receptive to the higher truths. As more and more recognize and accept the truth, this will accelerate acceptance by the masses. You will not find that everything will change overnight. Things may change very rapidly, but change will not happen all at once. And at the very end of the age,

159

you will find those who oppose change, and truth, who are absolutely adamant in their refusal to accept that which has by then become obvious to most. Even now, for example, some people upon Earth still insist that the Earth is flat! One simply cannot reconcile such illogic. It is caused by grievous errors in the soul pattern of such individuals and they must eventually recognize and correct these errors themselves."

"El Dorado, I wish that my wisdom would be as great as yours, someday."

"It shall be one day, Joseph. Remember, you are a Christed One. Soon, this Christ consciousness will increasingly manifest itself within your mortal consciousness."

"Can I hasten this process in any way?"

"Yes, by seeking and following the 'narrow way'. You are making progress. Soon, more doors will open to you. Ask and you shall receive, seek and you shall find, knock and it shall be opened unto you. Do not be anxious or afraid. Remember to maintain the simplicity of the little child. This does not imply simple-mindedness, but rather the certain knowledge that your Father will reveal Himself to you in all things that you earnestly seek."

"Thank you, El Dorado, for your beautiful and profound advice.

"What is that magnificent building over there that dominates the area adjoining the spaceport?"

"That is the administrative headquarters for the showcase of this entire solar system. This building houses the orientation center and central communications.

"All visitors are taken to this building upon arrival. Those from other planets in our solar system who are to become residents here are then taken to the planetary area of their origin for further orientation and assignment. Those who have arrived from Saturn and the other planets within our system as tourists, rather than residents, are given special briefing and are assigned accommodations here for their stay. Visitors from outside our solar system are likewise welcomed and briefed here. They are then offered whatever hospitality in our entire solar system that they are qualified by their level of ability to experience.

160

"You can now appreciate the excitement and anticipation that everyone feels upon arriving here, Joseph."

"I certainly can. The last time I can remember feeling this way was when my parents took me to the state fair for the first time! Only that cannot begin to compare with this experience."

"In addition to the planetary exhibits, which may take weeks or months to explore, you will find here the most elaborate and fantastic entertainment complex in the solar system. The greatest entertainers from within and without our solar system appear regularly. There are entertainment forms here that those of Earth have not conceived of in their most far-fetched imagination. Moreover, the camaraderie experienced here would be beyond description to an Earth person. The reasons for this are many, Joseph.

"First of all, only persons of goodwill and understanding are ever permitted here as visitors. Second, the law of attraction works to draw those souls who are old friends to visit here at the same time, thereby renewing many friendships that may be eons old. Third, no matter how highly evolved one becomes, there is always great excitement in new discoveries, new friendships, satisfying curiosity about other places, etc. Fourth, the very excitement and goodwill generated here has totally permeated the surrounding atmosphere with the most powerful and pleasing thought forms that activate and stimulate the most pleasurable emotions within one. Fifth, the love which one shows towards others is readily perceived and reciprocated, thus encouraging many new friendships.

"In this kind of an atmosphere open communication comes easily, and as you can see, it exists as naturally between man and animal as between men.

"*The more highly evolved one becomes, the more one realizes that communication is the most important thing in the universe. The whole concept of a center such as this is to maximize the communication process. As every type of being evolves, the communicative capacity is heightened, along with the awareness of the need to communicate. With the heightening of the communicative capacity comes a gradual recognition of the divine life force within everything. The recognition of this*

161

divine life force produces a growing rapport with Universal Mind.

"For example, Earthmen are not accustomed to thinking of animals as having souls or of being capable of mental communication. On the more enlightened planets, man knows better. Here on Saturn, for instance, man lives in peaceful and understanding coexistence with the animal kingdoms, resulting in an open and mutually respectful love and communication.

"With the gradual evolution of a planet into the fourth dimensional vibration, a change occurs in the animal population as well as the human population, whereby predators are eliminated and replaced by higher life forms. Such a change is now occuring on Earth. Some new animals have already been introduced, much to the amazement of Earthman. More will follow. Gradually, more and more people will become aware as whole species become extinct and new species appear out of 'nowhere'. There will also be some instances of behavior modification within existing species from a lower to a higher level of manifestation and conduct. This is all part of the cosmic communication process whereby beings evolving more slowly are grouped together by the law of attraction and the faster evolving are likewise drawn together.

"No being is ever lost in this process unless they are totally and permanently unyielding in their refusal to evolve. It simply involves a change of location from time to time. Those beings upon Earth who refuse to evolve into the higher vibrations of the fourth dimension and beyond, will be removed from this solar system altogether and taken to another place. There they will continue to suffer from the consequences of their stubborn ignorance for perhaps millions of years until they eventually choose a higher path of expression."

"I must admit, El Dorado, that I never before paid much attention to animals, much less to other life forms. After the beautiful experiences that I have had here and on Venus, however, my attitude has changed. In the future I will attempt to communicate with the divine life force within everything. I thank you for awakening me."

"The whole purpose of this journey, Joseph, is to awaken you to the realities of cosmic life. We recognize

162

that it is mostly ignorance that produces warped and negligent attitudes in Earth. When men of good will become aware, they invariably choose the higher path.

"The next phase of our journey is going to be of considerable interest to you. It concerns conditions of which we have not yet spoken."

"I truly regret that the time has come for us to leave here, El Dorado, yet I know that we must. It has been so enlightening and so delightful! Nevertheless, I am prepared to move on. I sense that we are now going to visit realms unseen by those on the physical or astral realms of expression. Am I correct?"

"Yes. Your perception is becoming very accurate, Joseph. This demonstrates that you are beginning to gain control of the technique of mind to mind communication via intuition as distinct from mind to mind thought projection.

"We are going to transport ourselves into the etheric level within our solar system. This is the level in which Christed beings normally abide, and this is the true heaven or nirvana of Earthly aspirations and scriptures. You are allowed to accompany me because you are a Christed being within your higher consciousness.

"To reach the Christ level of vibration and awareness will entail speeding up the electron movement within your atomic structure until it surpasses the speed of light. This is one of the powers of Christhood. Since you have not yet mastered this ability in your present embodiment and consciousness, I will control the change for you. The experience will be similar to the one in which we separated you from your physical body. I will embrace you within my aura."

The feelings, emotions and mental impressions that accompanied this change of dimension are totally beyond mortal description, except to say that the change from astral to Christ vibration far exceeded the change from physical to astral in joy, in awareness, in ecstasy, in euphoria, in an all-encompassing feeling of fulfillment and total happiness and well-being.

CHAPTER 12

An Extraordinary Interlude—Part III
To Orion And Back
Above Earth In A Giant Spacecraft

"Now that I am in this new consciousness, El Dorado, my degree of awareness is far greater. I know that you and I are going to travel aboard an etheric spacecraft, even though that seems strangely inconsistent with my mortal concepts of the christ realms of expression.

"At my present level of awareness, I can understand how convenient a spacecraft is, even for Christed beings, as a gathering place for meetings or as a means for large groups of beings to travel vast distances together. In fact, it makes far more sense than my former nebulous ideas of 'heaven'."

"You are right, Joseph. You and I are going to teleport ourselves aboard an etheric command spacecraft which is preparing for a brief journey to the constellation Orion. At this moment, the spaceship is anchored here above Saturn awaiting us. Come, let us go aboard."

El Dorado and I then left Saturn and rapidly approached the spaceship. As we reached the craft, I was amazed at its size. It was literally the size of a city, and as I soon discovered, it had all of the facilities of a city. I expressed my amazement to El Dorado and he replied:

"There are many, many craft in our galaxy that compare in size to this one. After all, our galaxy is a very big place, with hundreds of millions of suns and planets and solar systems. It requires craft this size and even larger to serve the purposes for which they are intended.

"This ship is able to move freely throughout the christ realms of the Universe. We have equipment on board that would completely boggle the minds of the scientists and engineers of Earth."

El Dorado then proceeded to show me around this totally fascinating space city, explaining to me those things which I could not readily perceive. It was a completely self-contained, self-sufficient environment.

As we moved about, I was continually and happily astonished as person after person approached us and greeted me by name. I was perhaps even more surprised when I recognized and greeted some of them! Never had I experienced such a feeling of belonging. Finally, we completed our tour and returned to the control room.

"Do you remember, Joseph, when I told you that communication is the most important thing in the universe? In the control center of any ship, you become very aware of it. In the control center of a large etheric craft, you cannot forget it for a moment!

"Through this communication center, we are in constant touch with all realms throughout the solar system and beyond.

"Behold, we begin our journey. As we do so, we place ourselves in communication with various points including our desination."

"How long will it take us to reach Orion?"

"We do not think of time so much in this dimension. It will seem to you a few minutes, perhaps the equivalent of fifteen minutes Earth time."

"That seems absolutely incredible, El Dorado. I can now comprehend travelling that fast in the astral or christ bodies, but it seems so impossible in any kind of spaceship."

"It would not seem so incredible, Joseph, if you thought of it in perspective. What we are dealing with is mind power. You have experienced how the power of the mind can transport your astral and christ bodies to the most distant destination in a mere moment by attaching a mental 'hook' to the point of destination and then reeling in, so to speak, at your own pace. The same principle is involved here in etheric spacecraft travel. After all, the spacecraft is but a vehicle which you are occupying. This vehicle is subject to the same laws as other vehicles which you occupy and which your mind can control!"

"I think I am beginning to understand."

"One of the purposes of this journey is to demonstrate to you that the speed of light does not limit the speed of mind, or the speed of travel. Observe, even now we approach the great nebula in Orion. Look and tell me what you observe."

"I see a most incredible panoply of stars, encased in what appear to be giant clouds of black, dark gray, rust, blue, red, green and white. It's like looking into an unbelievably gigantic cave. In the center of the cave is the Trapezium, which seems to illuminate the interior clouds with blue-white light. This must be the most breathtaking sight in the universe. This unbelievably immense cave is

168

lined with the most brilliant and fascinating jewels whose colors defy the spectrum."

"Listen carefully, Joseph, and remember everything that I am telling you now. Understanding will come later.

"Orion represents the Mighty Hunter of the skies who waged war against God, and was consequently bound with chains to the firmament of heaven. As you can see, the nebula is located in a position that corresponds to the loins, or the sacral, sexual area of the hunter.

"Now, I call your attention to that greatest book of nuclear physics, the Bible, Job 38:31-33,

Canst thou bind the cluster of the Pleiades,
    or loosen the bonds of Orion?
Canst thou bring forth the Mazzaroth in their season,
    or canst thou guide the Bear with her train?
Knowest thou the ordinances of the heavens;
    Canst thou establish the dominion thereof in Earth?

"The bonds of Orion represent the animal forces in man that seem to bind him so strongly to the flesh. The time has come for mankind to understand the secret of loosening the bonds of Orion. Man is beginning to sense the divine forces that are expressed through the sexual faculty, but as yet is ignorant of the proper use and control of these divine forces.

"The cave of the nebula symbolizes the activity that takes place in the sacral, sexual area of one's body. It is here in the cave or pit that stars must be born, later to rise in all their brightness and glory into the heavens (i.e., one's head) to glorify the lord (law). As each new star is born and rises to take its place in the diadem, there comes increasingly greater light and enlightenment to the individual until he shines with the brilliance of the sun, the Son of God, a Christ, even as Jesus!

"And how does one bring about this miracle of transcendence, Joseph? Be patient yet awhile and a master will come to reveal to you this greatest of universal secrets.

"Know this, my son, there is now upon Earth the master of masters, who has come again in Earth form and flesh, to show the way. He has come as any other man has come, through the womb of woman. His revelations will soon confound those who look for a more fanciful concept of salvation. You will be drawn to him, Joseph. At first you will not comprehend the nuclear dynamics of his revelations. Later, you will be one of two individuals in Earth who truly understands. Later still, many will come to join you in preparing Earth and mankind for the fourth dimensional experience.

"Remember this, that the study and comprehension of the heavens brings with it the understanding of one's self. As one loosens the bonds of Orion, one acquires the powers to guide one's own destiny!

"And now, we return to our solar system. We will leave this ship and the christ realms and return to the environment of Earth.

"I have been in mental communication with a command ship from Venus that is assigned to Earth under the command of St. Germain and his forces. They are concentrating on the American hemisphere in order to raise the level of consciousness. Let us be on our way. They are expecting us."

El Dorado again embraced me and we were transported by his mind to a large spaceship anchored above the Eastern seaboard of the United States. Enroute, my vibration was decelerated to the frequency of the astral body. Suddenly, we were in the control room of the spaceship.

"Welcome aboard our ship El Dorado and Joseph. We are honored that you are able to visit us on your journey."

"Thank you, Jandeen. We feel privileged to be with you. Joseph and I will be with you but a short time, but I wanted him to have the experience of being aboard a spaceship that was actively participating in the Divine Plan to raise the consciousness of the people of Earth."

"I also feel extremely privileged to be here with you, Jandeen. Soon, I must return to the heavy atmosphere of Earth to resume life in my physical body. I must savor every moment and every experience in the meantime so that I will have strong memories to sustain me for the trials that surely lie ahead.

"Would you give me some insight into how you are able to influence the level of consciousness of mankind upon Earth without violating man's free will?"

"Communication and love are the keys, Joseph. We communicate primarily on the subliminal level through the subconscious mind. On this level, we give suggestions to individuals so that they are inspired to complete specific tasks and goals. Other individuals, awakened to higher levels of awareness and receptivity, are directed by suggestion to perform activities willed by their own Higher Selves.

"Mostly, we communicate with individuals while they are asleep. Often, in their sleep, they are brought aboard our ship in their astral bodies where they are instructed to do those things which their own Higher Selves desire. In most instances the memory of this experience is prevented from reaching the conscious mind upon awakening. However, this does not materially diminish the effectiveness of the procedure. It simply prevents those who are not quite ready on the conscious level to accept us or our methods, from being traumatized and from rejecting our teachings while conscious.

"As you already know, the process of unlearning is very painful for most people. We try hard to spare people as much pain as possible under the circumstances.

"In conjunction with this procedure, we have equipment aboard our ship that monitors individuals and groups of all sizes and measures the temperature or pattern produced by the thoughts of their conscious minds. Through this monitoring capability, we are constantly aware of the effectiveness of our efforts.

"We also have the most sophisticated equipment aboard capable of changing the level of vibration. We can use this equipment to change the vibration of our ship so that we can be manifested in the physical vibration of any planet. Occasionally we lower our vibration so that anyone in Earth who might be looking in our direction can see us. Usually we are not low enough in altitude to be clearly perceived. We do this because our ship is so large that it would surely frighten most observers from Earth. However, at night we can frequently be seen as a 'star' in the sky. There have been many nights, Joseph, when you have seen us and recognized that we were not a star, but a spaceship.

"As you know, spaceships like ours are visible around the planet Earth at all times, and can often be seen by anyone interested enough to observe the stars at night. This in itself is one of the major ways that we are able to influence the level of consciousness. This was even prophesied in your scriptures as a sign of the latter days or the end of the age (referring to 'signs in the skies'). (See Gospels of Mark 13:25-26 and of Luke 21:25-28)

"Our equipment for changing vibrations is also used for altering the vibration of Earth. This is a very slow and deliberate process taken in cooperation with other spacecraft stationed all around Earth. The greatest of care and control is exercised to insure that the rate of change be uniform on both the physical and the astral planes. You have already experienced the consequences of this in your spiritual awakening!"

"Do you mean that you were actually monitoring and assisting me from this ship, Jandeen?"

"Yes, Joseph. We helped influence the thoughts and the studies that contributed to your awakening!"

"I'm impressed! Tell me Jandeen, why don't you communicate with the people of Earth through the conventional Earth methods of radio and television?"

"I'm sure that you have already figured out the answer to that question, Joseph. If we tried to communicate in this manner, it would probably be treated as a hoax, or else it would produce great fright. But there are other important reasons as well. We are concerned with developing the spiritual or psychic abilities of mankind. Our major efforts are directed to awakening these capacities in man of Earth. If we communicated freely on the mechanistic level, then it would not be likely that many would bother to develop their psychic abilities. It is these abilities that will eventually enable mankind to comprehend the truths that will dispel his ignorance. For example, how many people in Earth do you think would believe you if you told them of this remarkable journey that El Dorado has taken you on? They wouldn't believe you because they cannot yet conceive of maintaining consciousness outside their physical bodies, much less conceive of human life on so many different planets and dimensions. It is the development of these psychic or spiritual abilities that will enable man to 'go within' himself and learn the truth about many things needed to

172

advance himself and Earth into the fourth dimensional consciousness.

"Lack of awareness has been responsible for producing much hostile behavior on Earth. The basic cause of this hostility is man's strong intellectual development with little or no psychic or spiritual development. Take for an example the appearance of our spacecraft on Earth. What is the reaction of the psychically unaided intellectual mind? Time after time men have sent fighter planes to intercept us and presumably to threaten or shoot us down. Reacting to us in this manner defies all logic. We obviously possess a technology far superior to theirs and capable of annihilating them. You would think that after a few futile attempts to intercept or capture us, they would try a different approach. To compound their poor judgment, they have made every effort to cover up our existence by issuing denials and absurd explanations of the incidents.

"Any perceptive mind would soon conclude that if our intentions were hostile, we would already have captured or destroyed Earth. Since it is obvious that this is not our intention, the next logical step is to find out why we are here. The logical way to find this out is either communicate with us or listen to someone who already has. Whenever any one of our Earth Channels has attempted to explain our presence and our intentions, they have met with ridicule and closed minds. Granted, the situation has been further complicated by disturbed persons seeking attention, who claim contact with us when no such contact occurred. Nevertheless, there are large numbers of responsible individuals, like yourself, whose integrity is above reproach, that should at least be heard with some degree of credibility. This is one area where the mass news media of Earth has been largely negligent.

"The story of extraterrestrial spacecraft and their purpose in visiting Earth should be the biggest news story of the century, indeed of Earth history. If the truth of what we are and why we are here were pursued half as vigorously as other news of far less consequence, mankind would know that our intentions were peaceful and purposeful.

"Soon, time will run out within the limitations of the Divine Plan, and contacts will have to be made regardless of consequences. In the meantime, we are doing all we can to soften the shock of that day.

"We also influence the consciousness of Earth by inventions, music, art and literature as well as by introducing new ideas in the discipline of law, medicine and science. There is really no field of endeavor in which we do not help mankind expand the frontiers of his consciousness. We do this primarily through thought projection to those individuals who are most capable and receptive.

"Keep in mind that we never impose our ideas on anyone. Consent is always given by the individual's Higher Self before we attempt to influence or transmit ideas. Does this give you a clearer idea of how we are able to influence man's consciousness without violating his free will?"

"Yes, it certainly does. Thank you."

"The time has come again, Joseph, when we must be on our way. Thank you Jandeen for your gracious hospitality and assistance."

"You are very welcome, my brothers. Peace be with you until we meet again."

* * *

We left Jandeen's ship, which was anchored in a stationary position above the central east coast of the United States, and orbited Earth several times. I was able to see many other giant spaceships anchored above every continent and every country, as well as a much greater number of smaller ones assisting the larger vessels. When viewed from the dimension from which El Dorado and I were manifested, we could see Earth surrounded by a symmetrical network of 'UFO's' diligently working to bring about those changes that would advance Earth and its inhabitants into the new age of enlightenment and understanding. This was a very reassuring feeling. I gave thanks for being able to participate consciously in such a great and noble undertaking.

"Where are we going next, El Dorado? I sense that we are not yet ready to return to the motel room."

"We are going to a place that has become very familiar to you in your dreams."

"You mean we are going to the secret treasure room in Columbia?"

"That's where we are going, Joseph. You will see the difference in being there astrally in a dream state and being there astrally in a fully conscious and aware state."

CHAPTER 13

An Extraordinary Interlude—Part IV

In The Secret Records Room
In Colombia

After we had orbited Earth several times to observe the network of spacecraft, we stopped in space directly above the secret rooms of Colombia. I saw that there was an unmanned spacecraft anchored in this spot. El Dorado explained to me that this vessel monitored the area. In the event of an intrusion, the monitoring equipment would automatically relay the information to a mother ship for further action. El Dorado informed me that all secret rooms are protected in this manner.

After this, we landed on Earth at the entrance to the rooms and entered.

"What a tremendous experience it is being here in this consciousness, El Dorado! It is as if I were here in my physical body, only I feel much better than I ever felt physically.

"Everything looks the same except that now I realize absolutely that this is a true experience, that it is really happening."

"Come, Joseph, let us stand in front of the great medallion and test your increased powers of perception. Tell me what you are receiving."

"Well, it's a strange sensation. I can look at any part of this medallion and I can read and interpret it. At the same time, it is almost as if the medallion were actually speaking to me. You might say it is like a combination of visual and auditory impulses working together to impress my conscious mind. It appears that each faculty is confirming and ratifying the other so that no mistake in interpretation can be made."

"Because of the crucial importance of your mission as the custodian of this great treasure, it is absolutely vital, Joseph, that you be able to correctly read and interpret the information on this medallion. Therefore, I want you to tell me whatever information is contained in any area of the medallion that I point to. Tell me what this says."

"That area tells where the secret records rooms are located all over the planet Earth."

"Correct. Now tell me where some of them are."

"In addition to this one, there is one in Brazil, one in the Yucatan Peninsula, three in the United States;

one in Arizona, one in North Carolina, and one in California. Then there is one in the Great Pyramid of Giza in Egypt, one in Greece, one in England, one in the Himalayas."

"That is enough. It is obvious that you are interpreting correctly. Can you pinpoint the exact locations of these rooms as well as say the secret words that must be spoken before entry can be permitted?"

"Yes, I can, but the instructions state that the secret words must not be spoken aloud except to actually gain entry. Otherwise, the power of the spoken word would be broadcast upon the ethers and would no longer be secret."

"You are doing very well. Have you any comment before we continue?"

"I do have a comment. Something has just become clear that has been puzzling me for a long time. It concerns the secret room in the Great Pyramid of Giza. I have long been aware that such a room was supposed to be located there. What puzzled me was the fact that it could never be discovered. I know that scientists and Egyptologists have worked for years to try and locate such a room. They used the latest scientific equipment and techniques including computers and cosmic ray detectors, but without success. I was beginning to wonder myself if such a room actually did exist. Now I can understand the degree to which these records rooms are protected and why. It would simply be disastrous for some of this information to fall into the wrong hands. If they had succeeded in discovering the room, the records might have fallen into the hands of the self-seeking or unscrupulous. I can see the absolute necessity of keeping these records out of the wrong hands!"

"That necessity will become even clearer in a moment, Joseph."

"What do you mean?"

"I am going to take you inside the records room that is concealed here. Study the medallion carefully and you will see that the secret word that opens the door to this records room is also there. You need not hesitate to speak the word aloud this time because the word will be changed to a new one before we leave."

180

I searched the medallion to find the secret word. When I finally found it, I spoke it aloud (I was able to do so even though I was in my astral body). No sooner had I spoken the word than the great medallion began to rotate on a verticle axis, leaving clear access to a large room behind it. El Dorado and I stepped inside.

The contrast in lighting between the two rooms was the first thing that struck me. Whereas the first room was well lit, it was nevertheless with a subdued type of lighting. The records room on the other hand was very bright and airy. This was all the more remarkable because the walls, ceiling and floor were of the same obsidian-like substance.

The room was ringed with a remarkable mural that gave the impression of movement and activity. The mural was suprisingly vibrant in color and texture and the eye was drawn to it compulsively to see what story it had to tell. It was quite easy to 'read' because it depicted man's life on planet Earth and showed the progress and decline of man's development up to the present. The mural itself was a record of man's experience upon the planet. The upper half of the wall space was occupied by the mural.

Beneath the mural, and also encircling the room, was a system of what appeared to be filing cabinets that were built into the walls. I sensed immediately that these contained the records. This was a natural assumption since I hadn't seen anything else that looked like it might contain records. I asked El Dorado if these were indeed the records and he said yes.

In the middle of the room and extending the length of it were a series of tables or platforms with models of the various planets mounted atop them. In the center of the room was a very large and striking orrery. An orrery is a mechanical device, with balls or globes of various sizes mounted on arms and gears, which illustrates the relative motions and positions of the different planets and their satellites with relationship to the sun, which is in the center. My immediate impression was that it was a model of our solar system. However, as I began to identify the nine planets, I was astonished to suddenly discover that there were ten planets. I asked El Dorado if this was indeed our solar system. He told me that it was and explained it to me.

"At one time, Joseph, our solar system had ten physical planets (as distinct from the invisible planets). The asteroid belt that lies between Mars and Jupiter was the location of the tenth planet, which was fifth in distance from the Sun.

"As man evolved on this particular planet, his intellectual progress far outstripped his spiritual development. Conditions eventually reached a point where the technology of destructive forces combined with greed for power, and resulted in a cataclysmic war that annihilated the planet.

"Today, the situation on Earth is disturbingly similar. That is why so much attention and effort is being focused on Earth to prevent such a tragedy from recurring in our solar system.

"As our solar system proceeds into its new Great Cycle Orbit, another physical planet will be born of our sun, again bringing the number of physical planets to ten, as represented in this orrery."

The models of the individual planets that were mounted separately on the other tables showed the geographical layouts of each planet in the fourth dimensional vibration in which human life is manifested. In other words, their surface was not as it would appear in three dimensional photography. I found these to be quite fascinating. I also found that the models of Venus and Saturn conformed to what I had just seen in my visit.

I noticed that there were three globes representing Earth. The first one showed the geographical distribution of land mass and water prior to the shift in axis that occurred thousands of years ago. The second showed Earth as it is today. The third, El Dorado told me, depicted Earth as it would appear at the end of the millenium following Jesus' return to the planet. This meant that there would be further changes in the land masses.

At the far end of the room was a machine which looked unfamiliar to me. Comfortable chairs had been placed in front of this machine facing away from the machine toward the opposite wall. I asked El Dorado what it was and he said he would show me. First he took me to one of the filing cabinets and opened a drawer. He took from the drawer a box about the size of a small pack of cigarettes. He handed me the box and told me to open it. As I did, I experienced a sensation of deja vu. I removed from the box what appeared to be a crystal about two inches long, three-quarters of an inch wide and three-eights of an inch thick. El Dorado took the crystal from me and told me to sit in front of the machine. He placed the crystal in the machine, turned the machine on and came and sat beside me.

"What you are about to see, Joseph, is how the great pyramid of Giza was constructed, and why. The symbolism, functions and meaning attributed to this wonder of the world will also be explained."

I sat spellbound as the room darkened and the space in front of our chairs became alive with colored three-dimensional activity. The machine turned out to be a laser holographic projector. The holographic images were somehow stored in the crystal, and the laser projector was able to register the stored images and show them as a perfect three-dimensional movie. Naturally, no movie screen was necessary, since the images were projected into the middle of the room.

El Dorado warned me that some of the information in the movie was not to be revealed yet. However, I can tell you a few things about it.

When first completed, the pyramid was entirely covered, except for the gold capstone, with white marble facing stones. Thousands of years later, these stones were removed by plunderers who had no idea of their purpose or function. These facing stones had carvings of precise sequences, and patterns of universal signs and symbols, as well as letter, word and number combinations. Although tradition has it that the carvings contained the entire knowledge of the previous age, this was not the case. Actually, the carvings were part of the total pattern of energy forces comprising the entire pyramid. The carvings themselves produced an energy, a vibration, a magnetic force field based on universal laws which man of Earth has not yet rediscovered. In addition to the energies generated by the carvings, the crystalline properties of the white marble, when combined with the energy inherent to the pyramid shape, served to produce a diversified energy force field capable of performing many functions. Among those functions were the following:

1. To control and balance Earth's natural physical currents by uniting these currents with their non-physical astral counterpart currents. These unified currents were in turn connected to the grid of energy links that unify all planets within the solar system. The purpose of these linkages is a bit too complex to be discussed here and is beyond the scope of this book.

2. To provide a transmuting energy force for the entire planet. The pyramid, with its crystalline white marble surface and a large crystal emplaced in the proper interior focal point, served as a gigantic crystal to both gather and store enormous energies. These energies were used as a power source as well as for transmuting purposes. At one time, the great pyramid was connected to other pyramids around Earth to provide a grid for generation and transmission of electrical energy. This was accomplished without wires.

3. To blend the terrestrial, three dimensional vibration, with the vibration of astral antimatter and thus create a doorway between dimensions through which entities could conveniently pass and be in a protected enviroment, while traveling to and from Earth.

4. To provide a beacon for interplanetary travelers.

5. To preserve the sacred records of mankind's entire history upon Earth, which are complete even up to the present day. The records are preserved in the records room (not on the facing stones as tradition relates).

There are functions of the great pyramid which I cannot reveal, others which I do not yet understand, and finally those of which I am ignorant.

The pyramid was not constructed by the crude methods often depicted in many reference books. It was erected by master builders and craftsmen using the lost arts of sonic levitation, laser quarrying and the esoteric knowledge of secrets governing the universal laws of causes. Furthermore the pyramid was not built as a tomb, and was never intended to be a tomb, unless one facetiously considers the records to be the interred.

"What did you think of the movie, Joseph?"

"I found it totally engrossing and fascinating. I would like very much to see another one if we have time."

"Do you have a particular preference?"

"If there is anything on the subject of spiritual or psychic healing, I would like to see that."

"I will go even further than that. I will show you a movie that demonstrates to a high degree, the successful combination of scientific principles and technology with the intuitive insights of psychic diagnosis. You have become aware through your studies, Joseph, that both sound and color can be used therapeutically. In this movie you will see these concepts applied scientifically. It will be of great interest for you to know that these methods were used in Atlantis over 26,000 years ago. You helped to develop these techniques and you were the one to preserve the information on this very crystal, just as you had a part in constructing the pyramid that we have just seen."

El Dorado then placed this second crystal in the holographic projector. I was even more excited this time because I could anticipate the thrill that was in store for me. My excitement was heightened even more by the knowledge that I had created this crystal myself in another embodiment so long ago.

The scene in the movie was a large, slightly rectangular room. The room was probably about 55 feet long by 50 feet wide. The movie explained that the room was as perfect acoustically as could be made. One could easily see that the ceiling and walls were designed with acoustics in mind. The room was all white, but because of the unique lighting there was no glare. Near one end of the room, midway between the two walls, was a laser holographic projector that was similar to the one we were using. At the opposite end of the room, but about 15 or 20 feet from the wall, was a platform about 4 feet above the floor. This platform was molded of clear plastic.

A patient was treated as follows. First a diagnosis was made to determine all of the symptoms of the illness. After these symptoms were analyzed and recorded, a study was made to determine the root cause of these symptoms. This study went beyond the capability of modern medicine. Atlantean doctors recognized the total interaction of the physical, mental, emotional and soul or subconscious aspects of a human being. They recognized the futility and folly of treating symptoms without understanding the underlying causes of the disease. They recognized, for example, that many diseases and imbalanced conditions were brought about by karmic patterns lodged in the subconscious mind of the patient. Diagnosis of the causes of the symptoms was conducted by highly gifted psychics who were able to read the soul (akashic record) of the patient, as well as by physicians skilled in the physiological and psychological aspects of a human being.

When diagnosis was completed to everyone's satisfaction, the patient was ready for treatment. Treatment consisted in applying the therapy of sound or color or both. This was determined by studying reference material compiled over a long period of time. Formulas had been developed for the treatment of many types of disease.

The patient would either stand, sit or lie down upon the clear plastic platform depending upon his condition. If he was to receive the color treatment, a gemstone of the appropriate color was placed in the laser and a holographic image was projected toward the patient, completely surrounding and bathing his aura in that color. If more than one color was required, this procedure was repeated for each color. The length of time of exposure was usually predetermined. The reason the patient was placed upon the raised clear plastic platform was to make sure that his entire aura was saturated in the color.

If necessary, sound was used in the therapy at the same time as the color projections. Otherwise, the sound preceded or followed the color as prescribed.

It should be noted that this method of healing was not used for every kind of illness. Many, many other techniques and refinements of the healing arts were employed. This apparently was a highly successfully method of treating many diseased conditions, however.

"Well, I must admit, El Dorado, that I was thoroughly engrossed in that movie. I could feel myself actually participating in it. Tell me, is there any other type or kind of record here other than the crystals?"

"Of course. There are books, charts, graphs, pictures and objects of various kinds. The first cabinet contains a complete index of all the records contained here as well as an index of records contained in the other records rooms. What else would you like to know?"

"You know me. With my curiosity, I'd like to see everything. I realize, however, that we have a time limitation. Are there any records here showing the exact location of valuable mineral deposits?"

"There certainly are. The location of all large deposits has been known and recorded for a long time. In addition, the cheapest and quickest methods of mining and extracting these minerals is also recorded here. If you were to tell modern man how these minerals were originally found, you would be laughed at."

"Why? How was the information acquired?"

"By cooperating with those beings who control the elemental kingdoms of Earth. The elemental kingdoms control the plant and mineral life of manifested creation. You know this, Joseph, from your studies of devas, elves, fairies, gnomes, dryads, pixies, leprechauns, sprites, nymphs, elementals and other creatures. These beings actually exist, of course, as you and I both know, and they are under the direction of the angelic kingdom. Since modern man has lost touch with the reality of these nature kingdoms, he tends to treat believers with scorn and contempt. Through contact with the angelic forces that control the Earth elementals, the locations of significant mineral deposits were cataloged and placed in the records for future reference."

"I must say, that is an incredible example of cooperation between man and the forces of nature."

"Yes, Joseph. Man was intended to supervise and control the elemental kingdoms. When, through his ignorance and misuse of power, man was forced to relinquish control of the elementals, the angelic kingdom assumed this control until man could again evolve to his rightful role.

"As part of the Divine Plan to again remind man of this heritage, certain light workers have been guided and inspired to re-create an active and productive relationship with the devic forces and the elemental beings. One example of this effort that is becoming well known can be found near Findhorn in Northern Scotland."

"I have heard of the work being done there, El Dorado."

"There are many examples around Earth of the Divine Plan unfolding, waiting for mankind to see, to recognize and to grasp. As you now realize, Joseph, all that is required is an open mind, a willingness to learn, a willingess to *unlearn*, and some honest effort.

"Now the time has come for us to return. I know of no one who has been privileged to see or to experience more than you have on this journey. With privilege, as you know, comes the responsibility of using and sharing this knowledge with mankind. You must apply discernment in this matter. Certain things cannot be revealed. However, you will be guided to reveal those truths which will be of greatest benefit to mankind at this particular time."

You cannot begin to imagine the pain and sacrifice that is required to return to an earthly body at this stage of Earth's development. After having experienced the freedom and joy of the astral and etheric realms, to have to return to the conditions of Earth was somewhat worse than being sentenced to solitary confinement. Never have I been more aware of the truth of the saying, 'greater love hath no man than one who lays down his life for his fellow man'.

I realized fully the difficult path that lay before me. I was aware of the necessity to reveal many of my experiences and of the skepticism that would greet such a revelation. These thoughts were softened somewhat by the assurance that some would believe and benefit from these truths.

Upon returning to the motel room, we hovered above my mortal body while I further contemplated the ramifications of my extraordinary interlude. With heart bursting with gratitude and love, I thanked El Dorado for this fruitful experience. I was suddenly aware of a totally unique and personal relationship with El Dorado which I could not yet quite comprehend. He, of course, was aware of my thoughts and emotions. He again surrounded and infused my aura with his own and transported me once more into that state of euphoria that is far beyond describing. I relaxed rapturously in his presence for some time. Finally, after what seemed like hours, I realized that my consciousness had reentered my physical body without my being aware of it.

There I was, sitting in my motel room chair, wondering if I had really gone through this incredible experience, and knowing for certain that I had. I gazed expectantly at El Dorado. I knew that he would leave in a moment, but that he had some important thoughts to communicate.

"Joseph, you will soon be ready to assume custody of the Treasure of El Dorado. If your identity becomes known to the world, you will be besieged with requests for funds. Many who seek your aid will be sincere and well-meaning, but many will be interested only in self-aggrandizement. Of those who are sincere in their service to others, there will be many whose efforts are misled and whose well-meaning interests are contrary to the proper development of the Divine Plan. You will therefore do well to begin planning now for an orderly administration of the affairs of your custodianship.

"It is important that you begin writing a book. Take the material which you have already prepared from the discourses and combine it with the experiences of your astral journey. Then complete the book with the discourses that are yet to come. Some things in your completed book may shock, horrify, repulse, sicken, anger, terrify or confuse many people. You must not let this deter you from your mission. Just keep in mind what you yourself have learned and experienced—unlearning hurts!

"The information contained in your book will serve to awaken many, many people around Earth to the realities that you now know. It will indeed change their cosmic understanding. It will also help many to realize that they are not alone in their quest to raise the consciousness of mankind. Through this awakening process, an informal, worldwide organization can perhaps be formed, and a new channel of communication can be opened to link the 'light workers' together in many cooperative efforts that will advance the Divine Plan immensely.

"Keep in mind that there are hundreds of thousands of highly evolved souls who are presently incarnated upon Earth in order to serve the Divine Plan. The majority of them are not consciously aware of it. When they read a book such as yours, it will stir their very souls. Many of them will say to themselves, 'I believe a lot of these things. I wonder if I am a light worker,' or 'I have never read or heard of these things before, but they have the ring of authenticity. Perhaps I am one of the light workers he is referring to', or ' I wish I was a light worker and could serve in such a noble undertaking', or 'I believe what this book says, but I am not good enough to be a light worker', and many other similar things. Let me say once and for all, whoever *wants* to serve the light and does their best to enlighten mankind to the eternal truths contained in your book, is a light worker, and is serving the Divine Plan!

"At this time, many are afraid to speak out about the truths that they may know or suspect, for fear of derision and censure, if not outright persecution. It is necessary that more leaders voice their convictions about these matters and it will give others the courage to speak out. Your book can be a catalyst in encouraging people to be more outspoken.

"Be prepared to be rejected, scorned, humiliated, vilified, persecuted, attacked by character assassins, or otherwise abused and misunderstood. You will be hurt more by fanatics who zealously defend their philosophy rather than practice it, than you will be by the heathen who makes no pretentions to godliness!

"Do not be concerned that you will have to turn down requests for financial assistance. It is not your purpose to fund causes. There are private foundations and government agencies that aid other worthy causes. The Treasure of El Dorado, if it is used at all, must be directed to the priorities of the unfolding Plan.

"Your energies as custodian must not be diffused by efforts not directly related to the Plan. Be singleminded in your dedication to educating people.

"From this point on, call me whenever you feel the need. My forces have been directed to respond to your every thought, word and deed, to insure that your direction is continuous and purposeful.

"Have you any questions, Joseph?"

"Yes, El Dorado, I have one. How will I know when I am ready to be custodian?"

"Of that moment you will have no doubt. That moment will be preceded by an all-encompassing realization that will obliterate all uncertainty from your mind! Now you must devote your attention to writing your book."

CHAPTER 14

Serapis Bey Speaks On
The Unity Of Matter And Antimatter

The Communication Factor

Dutifully following El Dorado's instructions, I went to work on my book. Actually, I did more thinking than writing. So much was happening in my life at that time that I could not seem to sit down and put it all together.

El Dorado came to me frequently through his vibratory presence, but did not communicate mentally. He began communicating by an intuitive process in which I 'read' his mind rather than he mentally projecting his thoughts to me. He would come into my aura, and I would recognize him through the unique vibratory effect produced in my mind, emotions and physical body, but he would remain silent as far as mental projections were concerned. Gradually, I became accustomed to this and I became highly sensitive to his mind.

In this manner El Dorado let me know that many things were being delayed in implementing the Divine Plan because of man's failure to accomplish certain goals. For this reason I did not have to rush with the book. He let me know that when it was time for the book to be completed, that the energy and the inspiration would be there to get the job done.

While I was re-reading the discourses one day, Serapis Bey came to me and forthwith delivered his discourse.

"Hello, Joseph. This is Serapis Bey.

"The time has come to explain to you the unity of matter and antimatter, and how this unity constitutes the communication factor of all creation. This is not a difficult concept to grasp.

"For the moment, let us define matter as any physically manifesting form of energy. Let us define antimatter as non-physically manifesting energy. Then let us define energy as mind, and mind as intelligent energy.

"Now let us look at the atom. The entire visible and invisible universe is made up of these invisible units. The atom is not really invisible, it is only invisible to the unaided mortal eye. The atom does, however, have an invisible antimatter counterpart which we will explain a little later.

"As we continue to examine an atom, what do we observe? We see a miniature solar system with the proton, neutron mass representing the sun and the electrons representing the planets orbiting around the sun. We find elementary particles which represent moons and comets and meteoroids and asteroids. This analogy, incidentally, will aid your Earth scientists in their efforts to understand the mysterious 'quark' that they are seeking. They should think of the quark in terms of a comet that occasionally appears within a solar system.

"What we do not find in observing the atom is the glue that holds this micro-unit together in the eternally viable form of an atom. The glue is antimatter mind energy.

"This mind energy interpenetrates and binds the atom together as your mind force holds your body together. You will recall El Dorado's discourse on the bodies of man in which he discussed the astral and other bodies. The atom, like man, also possesses nonphysical, spiritual counterpart bodies which are immortal, and which we can call mind energy. It is this mind energy that gives the atom a divine life force which is inextinguishable. It is this divine life force that endows the atom with identity, intelligence, instruction for performance, and an insatiable thirst for knowledge coupled with a limitless capacity to draw knowledge from all other atoms with which it is connected. In the cosmic sense, this atom is connected to all other atoms by antimatter mind glue. Therefore, all knowledge is potentially available to every atom within the cosmos, as I will explain.

"Now let us proceed beyond the single atom and look at a unified family of atoms. For the sake of illustration, let us look at a life form which man considers simple and minute, the one-celled amoeba. The amoeba is a highly complex assembly of atoms of many varieties, functions and vibrations, which are uniquely combined to form an individualized expression of life. While each atom within the amoeba has the individual atomic qualities already described, there are other qualities in each atom of the amoeba which make each atom distinctly amoebic. Those qualities are the invisible antimatter mind energies which interpenetrate the amoeba atom.

"Holding the amoeba together is an amoebic mind life force which transcends the life force of the individual atoms, but includes all of the atoms within the amoeba. Every atom within the amoeba is inextricably intertwined with all of the other atoms within the amoeba through this antimatter mind energy and depends upon this amoebic life force to give it identity as an amoeba. Any force which affects a single atom within the amoeba affects every other atom within the amoeba through the automatic communication factor of the unifying amoebic mind energy force.

"From the amoeba, let us next examine an infinitely more complex unified family of atoms; a human being.

"Again recalling El Dorado's discourse to you regarding the various bodies or aspects of a human being, let us look at the whole person. You can readily comprehend that you are an almost inconceivably large aggregate of atoms. If we are to let each atom in your body represent a solar system, we would find that your body consisted of literally countless galaxies, universes and multiverses. From the frame of reference of a single electron orbiting its proton neutron sun in a single atom inside your physical body, an observer standing on the electron, like a human being standing on Earth, could not possibly conceive of the extent of the multiverses that comprise your entire body! Such an observer could not begin to grasp the shape or form of your total unified body of which his electron planet is an integral, though minute, part. Your body would simply be too vast for any one to make out its shape or form from such a tiny point of reference. And yet, a tiny pin prick in the toe of your multiverse body is instantly perceived and felt in your brain which seems infinitely distant in the microcosmic scale to the observer standing on that tiny electron planet.

"How was the impression and the pain and the sensation of the pin prick instantly transmitted to the brain? This transmission was accomplished through the antimatter energy body which interpenetrates and connects all atoms within the unified individualized body!

"The speed of this transmission is instantaneous. There is no limit to the speed of mind. Wherever individualized mind exists, thought energy is transmitted instantly between any two points within the unified family of atoms that constitutes the individualized mind entity.

"The largest unified family of atoms is that all-encompassing intelligent mind energy force identified and referred to as God, or Universal Mind, or Father-Mother God, etc. Every individualized consciousness as well as every atom, both physical and non-physical, both matter and antimatter, exists within the one unified family of atoms of the God Being. Therefore, all things, both manifest and unmanifest, are a related, interconnected, integral part of God Mind or Universal Mind.

Now you can more easily comprehend what it means to say that 'we are all one'. We are all indeed part of the One great Whole. We are totally and permanently a part of Universal Mind.

"Once we recognize that we are an integral, intelligent part of the whole, we have reached a point where it is possible to become consciously unified with Universal Mind.

"At this point we need to understand the method of uniting consciously with Universal Mind. How is it accomplished? To simplify, we can say that it is done by increasing the vibration frequency of our individualized mind body. The higher the frequency we can generate in our mental body, the greater the knowledge and understanding available to us from Universal Mind. The greater the knowledge and understanding available to us, the higher we can tune our frequency. You might compare the process to a radio receiver. A cheap, simple receiver will pick up broadcasts from only a few radio stations. Although there are literally hundreds and thousands of continuous broadcasts of varying frequencies, the unsophisticated receiver is capable of receiving but a very few.

"A more sophisticated instrument, by contrast, is capable of discriminately selecting from a much greater number of broadcasts, with a much higher range of frequencies, affording the listener a much wider scope of knowledge and information.

"Universal Mind encompasses a limitless range of frequencies and continuous broadcasts. The more developed and perceptive an individualized mind becomes, the greater the frequency range within Universal Mind that consciousness can tune in to.

"At all times, it should be understood that all knowledge exists within our personal unified individualized family of atoms. Accordingly, we never have to look outside of our own selves for any knowledge or understanding. Within every single atom throughout all of creation, the totality of Divine Mind exists, waiting to be recognized, understood and communicated with!   *

"Only one thing more needs to be explained to you, Joseph, about communicating with Universal Mind. That is the manner in which one's frequency is raised so that one can tune in to a higher level of knowledge and understanding. The answer to the secret is love! Love is the answer!

"I will leave you now to ponder awhile. Soon will come another master to deliver a final discourse to unlock your door into the fourth dimension and beyond.

"I will leave you now, but I am really not leaving you. For as you now understand, *we are one,* locked together securely within the unified family of atoms of Universal Mind for all eternity. Glory be to God, and to the God within every atom of creation, and to the God within you and within all men and within everyone and everything always and forever. I love you."

CHAPTER 15

San Cha Speaks On
Sex

The Nuclear Dynamics Of Cosmic Sex

Sex Unlocks The Atomic Secrets
Of Universal Mind

The Great Apostasy

To say that I was anxiously awaiting the final discourse in my training would be a great understatement. While I still could not totally comprehend the complete significance of what being custodian of the Treasure of El Dorado would entail, I was nevertheless eager to take on this new responsibility.

Looking back on it, I was reminded of the saying, 'Fools rush in where angels fear to tread'. If I had fully understood, even at that advanced stage of my training, what was really involved in this awesome responsibility, I might not have been in such a hurry. In fact, I might have wanted a bit more time to take it easy, relax and enjoy some mundane pleasures for awhile.

I was not given the time to do any relaxing. El Dorado came to me shortly thereafter.

"The time has come in your training, Joseph, to reveal to you the greatest secret that can be given to mankind at this stage of his evolutionary development upon Earth. This secret concerns the so-called human sexual faculty. Sex is at once man's greatest, but least understood, gift.

"Opinions on the proper use or non-use of sex have caused mankind untold misery and suffering through the ages. Besides suffering, there has also been great bewilderment. Man has simply not been able to reconcile the conflict between ignorance and guilt struggling against nature's strongest drive to balance itself.

"Accompanying me today to deliver this discourse is San Cha. San Cha is recognized and loved throughout every realm of our solar system as a great scientist and cosmic teacher. At this point, Joseph, I will remove my vibration from your aura in order that San Cha may enter and begin this important instruction."

"Joseph, my beautiful and steadfast friend through eternity, you know me by many names. I will not tell you any of these names at this time. As your level of consciousness continues to rise, you will know me.

"First, you must remember what El Dorado told you in the beginning. Unlearning hurts! What I have to say to you about the cosmic realities of sex will startle and amaze you. It will not be in accord with anything that you have learned, or that man-made religion or immoral 'morality' teaches. Nevertheless, we are confident that you will accept this knowledge in an openminded manner and think it through to its correct conclusion.

"These are the end days, the latter days of Scripture, where we must deal with all things out in the open. Those who cannot work with truth, who cannot open their minds and their hearts to cosmic laws and realities, have only themselves to blame for whatever consequences befall them. God, indeed, knows that we are doing our utmost to save man from his own ignorance, and from his blind obedience to a warped subconscious mind. In the end, and this is the end, there is only so much that we can do. The rest is up to man himself.

"For centuries the pendulum has swung in the direction of sexual ignorance, and repression, taboos, intimidation, fears, reliance upon authority figures to circumscribe sexuality, and so forth. Invariably, the authority figures themselves have all been grossly ignorant regarding the true nature of man's sexuality.

"In Earth's twentieth century the pendulum has swung closer to the opposite extreme in a balancing effort to extricate man from his sexual hangups. The opposing swing of the pendulum has been a necessary compensatory reaction to enable man to break free. Neither end of the pendulum's swing represents a balanced condition. Balance is achieved at a point midway between the extremes.

"Now the time has come for balance and for true understanding.

"Now the time has come for authoritative guidance in exercising this most precious faculty. And where should one turn for such guidance? To the sacred Scriptures, Joseph. It is there that one will find the most precise, comprehensive and authoritative information and guidance available in Earth!

"However, a major obstacle prevents the individual from being able to do this. No one can interpret the cosmic meaning of Scripture without being in a state of cosmic consciousness. The sacred Scriptures were never intended to be interpreted for the masses before now, because the sacred knowledge would have been profaned by unprepared mankind. But in these end days, all must be revealed regardless of the consequences. Accordingly, the Scriptures themselves state that someone will be sent in the end days to unravel their mysteries.

"When the Scriptures have been interpreted correctly, man will realize the truth of what Sananda has told you in his discourse. Do you remember what he said, Joseph?"

"Yes, San Cha, I remember vividly. He said, 'The Bible is a scientific treatise on nuclear physics, written in a universal metaphysical language, which details the precise formula for attaining cosmic (christ) consciousness'."

"Excellent, Joseph! That is exactly right. Believe me when I tell you, there is now one incarnated in Earth who is performing this role of interpreting the Old and New Testaments. You know him. He knows you. The universal law of attraction has brought you together to cooperate in this cosmic drama to release man of Earth from his ignorance.

"The irony of all this, and one of the difficulties of the task will be man's probable unfortunate reaction to this priceless information. Whoever presents the information can expect to be hated, despised, scorned, mocked, ridiculed, ignored, maligned, persecuted and otherwise abused by Earth's 'enlightened' religious leaders, moralists, and Pharisees. Does this seem like a replay of 2,000 years ago when the same thing happened to Earth's greatest Teacher?

"Don't worry too much about all of these negative reactions, Joseph. During the intervening 2,000 years the pendulum of ignorance has worked its way back closer to a center position. Accordingly, you will find many beautiful, enlightened, loving, caring, thinking and knowing souls who will join in, and help, who will intuitively understand what we are trying to do, and who will accept the leadership of 'Him who is to come'.

"What has sex to do with cosmic consciousness? What has nuclear physics to do with sex? How does one use and control one's sexual capacity in this mysterious process?

"These, and all other questions dealing with this subject will be answered through the forthcoming interpretation of Scripture. This interpretation will first appear as a record, later as a newspaper. Both of these will be rejected, misunderstood, misintepreted and forgotten by those who receive them. Still later, a book will be written in a strange style and structure setting forth the cosmic truths hidden in universal code language in the Scriptures. This book may at first be rejected by publishers for being too cryptic. If so, later circumstances will compel its publication.

"The person upon whom the responsibility to interpret the Scriptures devolves, is required to be in a state of cosmic consciousness so that he can understand and translate the hidden meanings contained therein. Because of this, his manner of expression may be different. In actuality, it is quite simple and easy to understand, but because it is different from what people are used to, it may require some concentration for the average person to grasp. If one tries to comprehend what is given, one will be rewarded with the pearl of great price.

"Again, referring to Scripture, the information contained in the Scriptural interpretations, will constitute the apostasy which must occur prior to the second coming of Jesus the Christ.

"Let no man be deceived regarding the seriousness of these words.

"Now, Joseph, I am going to explain to you the sacred mysteries of the divinity of sex. Please do not use this information in your book except in a very general way. This is not your role to perform at this time. Your present role is to teach mankind about the overall Divine Plan which has been given to you."

San Cha then explained to me in great detail the beautiful and sacred use of mankind's priceless gift of sex in attaining cosmic (christ) consciousness. I understood the nuclear dynamics of cosmic sex, and how it erases the conflicts presently existing within everyone's body that prevent the unification of atoms within one's being. I further learned how this atomic fusion within one's being releases the secrets that are locked within every atom. I understood how this fusion changes the frequency vibration of one's mental body which enables one to tune in to Universal Mind. I learned that this was a gradual process and that it might take years for some to complete. I learned that one should not even commence this process until they were in a state of excellent health. I learned that the terms 'crucifixon' and 'resurrection' have nothing to do with dying on a wooden cross and 'rising up to heaven' after death, but are instead terms describing the nuclear results of this mysterious process that involves 'crossing over' into a state of being 'reborn' in a newly transformed fourth dimensional body. I learned that when one was fully 'reborn' in the new nuclear body, one would be immune to death and disease in the conventional sense. I learned that the 'beast' in the Book of Revelations whose number is 666 was in reality the carbon atom of which every human being is constructed— 6 protons, 6 neutrons, 6 electrons. It is this beast, these atoms of which you are constructed, which must be conquered in order to rise up incorruptibly into immortality.

I learned many, many, many more wonderful things that were awaiting man when he released himself from the ignorance and errors of the past. Just as San Cha had warned me, I was both startled and amazed by these unbelievable revelations. I faithfully recorded the discourse.

I then began a thorough and objective analysis of my life experiences that had led me up to this point. I carefully studied and restudied all of the discourses as well as the most authoritative channelings in my library. I came to the conclusion that everything that I had received and that I had experienced leading up to these incredible revelations had been to prepare me to understand and accept San Cha's discourse.

Of course, the ultimate test of anything eventually boils down to the practical question, 'does it work?'. If it doesn't work, the most brilliant discourse in the world will not give it validity. If it does work, the most intense opposition in the world cannot prevent its eventual acceptance.

Does it work?

CHAPTER 16

*Joseph Attains Self-Realization
And Becomes Custodian Of
The Treasure Of El Dorado*

I have finally come to the realization of who I AM!

I AM a fully developed personality temporarily residing in planet Earth in a flesh and blood body. This personality was instituted at the discretion of my own Higher Self for the purpose of expanding and evolving Itself through a continuing myriad of evolutions and involvements. At this point, this personality and consciousness that is Joseph, recognizes that it is but one personality and consciouness of a much vaster total Self.

I can now look at all of the other personality developments that I AM and say with recognition, "I AM THAT".

I can look, for instance, at the many life episodes that I have experienced in Earth and elsewhere, and I can see in each one how a personality evolved and developed, shaped by the destinies and experiences of certain particular places or dimensions. I can recognize that each personality development is an individualized consciousness for all eternity, and yet is completely connected with each other personality development of my total Self.

Having reached this point of realization, I can at any given moment be whomsoever I wish to be of the many personalities that I AM. I can therefore tune in to whatever knowledge, ability, experience, aptitude or awareness that exists within any of these personalities that I AM. Beyond this, I can also communicate with Universal Mind through my superconscious vibration.

It's like looking at a roomful of men and women with an extraordinary range of talents, abilities and experiences, and being able to say to each one, "I AM you," and "You are me". And each one in the room knows and appreciates and loves each other one with the full realization of "I AM YOU"! I might with equal ease look upon the whole human race, the whole of mankind, upon all of creation, and say with absolute realization, "I AM YOU"! For I now recognize the Divine Life Force which binds and sustains us all as ONE, and of which I AM an ETERNAL, integral, intelligent, functioning part.

I now realize who I AM!

I AM THAT I AM!

I AM ONE with my High Self, I AM ONE with the God Force!

THE FATHER AND I ARE ONE!
My High Self is El Dorado!
I AM EL DORADO!!!!!!
I AM the Custodian of the Treasure of El Dorado!

Arise, Eagles!

Arise, 144,000,
The Eagle flies
You are the Eagle,
Arise! Arise!

The hope of Earth,
The hope of Man,
The risen Atlantis
Where it all began.

The land of the Eagle,
Its symbol is one,
The risen Atlantis
of the Western Sun.

The hope of Earth,
The hope of Man,
The Bicentennial
Of a Plan.

If you Eagles fail
To heed this call,
The result will be
Neanderthal!

If you Eagles fail
To leave the nest,
There's scant hope
For all the rest!

By El Dorado
2-13-76